NIS/NCIS SAN DIEGO

HISTORY OF THE NAVAL INVESTIGATIVE SERVICE AND NAVAL CRIMINAL INVESTIGATIVE SERVICE IN THE SAN DIEGO REGION

BY NCIS SPECIAL AGENT ALLAN SIPE, RET.

Green Ivy Publishing
1 Lincoln Centre
18W140 Butterfield Road
Suite 1500
Oakbrook Terrace IL 60181-4843
www.greenivybooks.com

NIS/NCIS San Diego/Allan Sipe

ISBN: 978-1-946775-95-5
Ebook: 978-1-946775-96-2

Contents

1
Preface

Over fifty years ago—in February 1966—the Naval Investigative Service (NIS) was created from the investigative resources of the Office of Naval Intelligence (ONI). When one stops to consider that NIS employees at that time must have been in their mid-twenties or older and now would be in their mid-seventies or older, and consider the attrition rate over those fifty years, one can surmise that there are not a large number of persons alive who were part of that February 1966 transition.

With substantial US Navy and US Marine Corps resources, the San Diego Region has been a center of ONI, NIS, and its follow-on organization the Naval Criminal Investigative Service (NCIS) presence since the early twentieth century.

To the writer's knowledge, the history of NIS/NCIS in the San Diego Region has never been documented.

The writer spent over fifteen years of his NIS/NCIS career in the San Diego Region and has resided here since his retirement. The writer knows many retired NIS/NCIS employees, many of whom have also remained in the San Diego area after retirement.

In March 2016, the Southwest Region NCIS Office and the Southwest NCIS Association Chapter of retirees combined to celebrate the fiftieth Anniversary of our organization. The writer presented the Keynote address, the subject of which was the History of NIS/NCIS in the San Diego Region. Out of this effort, the writer decided to document the NIS/NCIS History in the San Diego Region while his generation and older retired employees of our organization are still alive. The writer designed a questionnaire which was disseminated to over one hundred retired employees, over sixty of whom have provided information reported in this publication. The writer wishes to thank these contributors who gave the best years of their lives to ONI/NIS/NCIS. Special thanks to twenty-three men—by the writer's count—who were employees of ONI when NIS was created (Plank Owners) and who honored me by contributing to this project.

Seals of ONI, NIS, NCIS

2
District Intelligence Office (DIO)

The Office of Naval Intelligence (ONI) was founded in 1882. In 1916, District Intelligence Offices or DIOs were established on the staffs of each Naval District Commandant and ONI became responsible for protection of the Navy against espionage, sabotage, and subversion. Naval District Headquarters were generally located in areas with a large navy or Marine Corps presence. Such was the case in San Diego--headquarters of the 11th Naval District—more recently called Commander Naval Base San Diego. DIOs were designated responsibilities to conduct criminal, counterintelligence, and personnel security or background investigations for the Department of the Navy (DON) which consists of the US Navy and US Marine Corps. Here in San Diego, the DIO was a Navy Captain or Commander who had a military and civilian staff that performed a wide range of intelligence and investigative functions. The DIO and staff were located at the foot of Broadway until the summer of 1964 when they relocated to Fordham Street.

On active duty in the Navy as a Yeoman First Class in 1952, Roy Mosteller was assigned to ONI conducting Personal Security Investigations (PSIs) in Long Beach, CA. In November 1953, he was hired under contract as an ONI Special Agent in the San Diego office at a salary of $4,050 per year. In those early years, ONI encouraged investigators to not talk openly about their work and suggested that they publicly identify themselves as Research Analysts. From 1953 to 1962, Roy and a few other agents handled all investigative work—mainly PSIs—in the 11th Naval District area of operations--Southern California, Arizona, and Southern Nevada. To do this job, there were about twenty-five or fewer Special Agents in the 11th Naval District—twelve or so in San Diego, six in Los Angeles, and three or four in Long Beach.

ELEVENTH NAVAL DISTRICT INTELLIGENCE OFFICERS

LT. CDR.	J. D. SMITH, USN	23 JUNE 1924	2 JUNE 1926
COMDR.	W. B. WOODSON, USN	5 JULY 1926	15 JUNE 1929
LT. CDR.	J. D. SMITH, USN	16 JUNE 1929	20 MAR. 1931
COMDR.	F. T. CHEW, USN	21 MAR. 1931	13 MAY 1933
COMDR.	J. H. EVERSON, USN	7 JUNE 1933	11 DEC. 1934
COMDR.	R. H. GRAYSON, USN	21 DEC. 1934	29 MAR. 1935
COMDR.	H. C. DAVIS, USN	23 APR. 1935	22 NOV. 1937
LT. CDR.	R. A. DIERDORFF, USN	15 DEC. 1937	13 MAY 1938
CAPT.	E. M. ZACHARIAS, USN	13 MAY 1938	8 NOV. 1940
CAPT.	B. L. CANAGA, USN (Ret.)	8 NOV. 1940	27 NOV. 1942
COMDR.	D. D. DOUGLAS, USNR	27 NOV. 1942	17 JAN. 1944
CAPT.	R. C. MAC FALL, USN (Ret.)	17 JAN. 1944	7 JUNE 1945
CAPT.	C. A. PERKINS, USNR	7 JUNE 1945	25 JUNE 1946
CAPT.	A. M. HURST, USN	25 JUNE 1946	15 JUNE 1948
CAPT.	T. J. SHULTZ, USN	17 AUG. 1948	2 JUNE 1951
CAPT.	L. T. MALONE, USN	14 JUNE 1951	25 OCT. 1951
CAPT.	J. K. WELLS, USN	23 DEC. 1951	24 OCT. 1955
CAPT.	J. M. WOOD, USN	20 OCT. 1955	17 NOV. 1958
CAPT.	EDWARD BRUMBY, USN	16 FEB. 1959	30 JUNE 1960
CDR.	J. M. DAVID, USNR	1 JULY 1960	1 MAY 1961
CAPT.	D. NASH, USN	1 MAY 1961	30 JUNE 1965
CAPT.	S. M. ZIMNY, USN	30 JUNE 1965	4 FEB 1966

11th Naval District Intelligence Officers

When hired, it was routine procedure for new agents like Mosteller to get trained by working alongside an experienced agent. ONI recognized the need for more formal training and initiated what became known as Agent Basic School. The first class convened in early 1954 in Washington, DC, and Roy Mosteller says he is privileged to have been a member of that first class.

Harry Stovall was hired as an ONI Special Agent in July 1963. The DIO was Capt. David Nash, USN. The civilian staff was led by Supervising Agent Bill Clayton, his assistant, Bill Poole, and San Diego Senior Resident Agent Pat Daly. Another Resident Agency was located in Los Angeles. As provided by Harry, the DIO Personnel Roster in 1963 consisted of: Capt. D. Nash, USN, Supervising Agent Bill Clayton; Assistant Supervising Agent Bill Poole; Senior Resident Agent Pat Daly; Special Agents Pete Alberse, Jim Beaupalant, Jim Byrd, Reece Freeman, Bob Grossman, Don Hartman, Bert vonMaucher, George Reis, Bob Steele, John Stevens, Al Turner, and Bob Usher. New agents hired in 1963 were Dick Childs, Fred Grim, Pat Kewley, Arnie Sleeper, and Harry Stovall

Pictured L to R are George Morse, Dale Kreymeyer, Roy Mosteller, and Vincent Haley.

Roy Mosteller, Harry Stovall, and most all ONI Investigators began their law enforcement career conducting PSIs, also called Background Investigations (BI). A PSI is a very thorough investigation concerning an individual to determine his suitability for a security clearance. Thus, aspects such as the applicant's character, associates, activities, finances, and loyalty are examined. This is done by examining public records including law enforcement, interviewing character witnesses, talking to neighbors, employers, and associates, all becoming an extensive collection of all the favorable and unfavorable information gathered concerning the applicant.

Although ONI offices in the early 1960s focused on PSI investigations, they also had other responsibilities. A Secretary of the Navy instruction clearly provided the authority to ONI to conduct criminal investigations and counterintelligence matters in the Department of the Navy.

In the late 1950s and early 1960s, San Diego agents were routinely sent on two week trips to cover PSI leads in Arizona and Nevada. On one of these trips, Roy Mosteller sought out a high school principal to interview regarding a young sailor who was assigned to an important and sensitive Navy position. When Mosteller named the subject of the PSI and told the principal that the sailor was assigned to the Presidential yacht Sequoia where he was in close proximity to President Eisenhower, the principal said, "The Navy doesn't know this sailor very well do they."

The principal then told Mosteller that as a youngster, the sailor was well known for his often extreme fits of temper and explained that as a teenager, the young boy got into an angry fight with another boy and had killed his opponent. Mosteller obtained a statement from his source, found the nearest pay telephone, and contacted his San Diego office. To this day, Mosteller has often thought about how quickly the Navy acted to transfer this sailor to other duties.

USS Sequoia was a former yacht used for Presidents from Herbert Hoover to Jimmy Carter. In 1933, Sequoia was transferred to the US Navy, where she was commissioned and given her USS status, serving officially as the presidential yacht. She was decommissioned as an official Navy vessel under President Roosevelt during WWII. From 1936 to 1969, Sequoia became the yacht of the Secretary of the Navy. During this period, Sequoia was also used by presidents and other high-ranking government officials.

When automobile manufacturers commenced putting seat belts in cars in the early 1960s, agents thought belts would be good to add to ONI's Navy cars, but Washington would not spend the money for them. Thus, Roy Mosteller and another agent went to Pep Boys, bought seat belts and spent several weekends installing them themselves. To Mosteller, it always seemed like ONI had a money problem.

By the mid 1960s, ONI was conducting more and more criminal investigations. For ONI to have investigative responsibility, the agency needed jurisdiction over the suspect(s), the crime itself, and the location in which the crime occurred. In simpler terms, the suspect (s) needed to be an active duty Navy or Marine Corps member or in particular circumstances, a civilian employee of the Department of the Navy. The crime had to be classified as a major crime under the Uniform Code of Military Justice which equated to a felony in other jurisdictions. And the crime had to be committed onboard a military installation in which the US Government had exclusive jurisdiction or shared jurisdiction with a state or local agency.

The investigative responsibilities of an ONI/NIS Special Agent have been compared to that of an FBI agent. In some respects, that is a correct comparison. But in the early years of our organization, an ONI/NIS agent was expected to handle just about any type of investigation assigned to him whereas in the much larger FBI, agents were able to specialize in specific fields. This meant that an ONI/NIS agent could be expected to cover the entire gamut of major crimes—from theft of government property to sabotage, from simple narcotics or dangerous drug possession to homicide, or from loss of a classified message to espionage.

Roy Mosteller recalls an investigation involving two men who had served as Communication Technicians (CT rating or cryptologists) in the Navy during the early 1950s. After their service, they both were employed by the National Security Agency in 1957 and defected to Russia in 1960. Since they had been assigned to the Naval Security Station in Imperial Beach during their Navy time, the ONI office was requested to conduct appropriate inquiries. Mosteller recalls difficulties in getting any information from their former associates because he was not a member of the "CT family."

George Reis was probably the San Diego office's first polygraph examiner. His career, including law school, started in the late 1940s with public law enforcement agencies, graduation from Keeler Polygraph Institute in 1958 and hire by ONI in 1959. As a Special Agent, he investigated all major crimes, was a forensic photographer/crime scene photographer, criminal interrogator, firearms instructor, and specialized in instrumental interrogation as a polygraph examiner. He was qualified by the National Rifle Association as a pistol expert, and firearms instructor and annually tested the San Diego agents for their firearms qualification. He was qualified for forensic photograpy by the Eastman Kodak School of crime scene photography.

Starting his employment at ONI, George was assigned as an office mate of Bob Steel--lie detection expert and an author of an interrogation and polygraph column in "Police Magazine." One day, Bob and George were working together on a theft case. Three suspects showed deception on the polygraph so they were scheduled for further interrogation the next day. That night, a gasoline Molotov cocktail was thrown into Bob and George's office. The fire department arrived quickly and not too much damage was done. Bob and George went to the place where the suspect sailors lived. All three had gasoline fumes in their mouths, having siphoned the gas for the bomb from an auto gas tank. They were arrested, confessed, and imprisoned.

After conducting several thousand polygraph exams, George retired from federal agent status in 1980. George has also become an artist of note, having recently painted portraits of many stars of the NCIS television show including Mark Harmon, Cote de Pablo and most recently Emily Wickersham.

Sunnie Smith Wilder and Mary Mitsias were hired by ONI in the early 1960s as Secretaries and Admin Support professionals. Both worked with numerous navy officers and senior agents at the Broadway, Fordham Street, and Federal Building NIS offices. Both completed long and distinguished NIS careers.

In February 1966, the name Naval Investigative Service (NIS) was adopted to distinguish the organization from the rest of ONI. Under the Director of Naval Intelligence, the new command consisted of three functional organizations: the Director NIS and his headquarters staff; Naval Investigative Service Offices (NISO); and NIS Resident Agencies (NISRA) which were the basic operating components. The local DIO, Capt. S. Zimny, transitioned into Commanding Officer NISO San Diego.

Harry Stovall was serving as one of five agents in Okinawa in early 1966 when he noted the only change was the new NIS sign on the office door. In those early years, Harry said that agents wore suits, carried a .38 cal revolver, drove a variety of high mileage vehicles passed down from Navy recruiters to ONI, and had to own a hat to wear at the four week Basic School. Harry related that forms used were Form 52 as Notice of Case Pending or Action/Lead Sheet and Form 119 as Report of Investigation. During an interrogation, Harry said that a secretary would take dictation, hand type a statement, and return it to the agent for the subject to review and sign.

Although investigative responsibilities transitioned from the DIO to the new NIS organization, Naval District Commanders and staffs continued to be supported by NIS. From his time in 1966 on the staff of the 11th Naval District through a later name change to Commander Naval Base San Diego to the end of the NISRO structure in about 1994, the Commanding Officer of the NISO also served as the Counterintelligence Officer on the Admiral's Staff.

Chart 2-1 11th Naval District Intelligence Office

DISTRICT INTELLIGENCE OFFICE -- 11TH NAVAL DISTRICT					
	DIO	SA	Asst. SA	AGENTS	ADMIN
Dec51-Oct55	CAPT J.Wells	C.Morehead		R.Mosteller, F.Reeves, H.Strolan,	
Oct55-Nov58	CAPT J.Wood	"		P.Daly, R.Freeman, J.Beaupalant,	
Feb59-Jun60	CAPT E.Brumby	"		G.Reis, R. Steele, W.Poole, L.Bee,	
Jul60-May61	CDR J.David	"		J.Byrd,W. GrayR.Grossman,	
May61-Jun65	CAPT D.Nash	W.Clayton	W.Poole	P.Daly, R.Freeman, J.Beaupalant,	S.Smith,
Jun65-Feb66	CAPT S.Zimny	"		P.Alberse, B.vonMaucher, G.Reis,	K.Fogelberg
				R.Steele, J.Stevens, A.Turner,	M.Mitsias
				H.Stovall, R.Childs, F.Grim,	
				J.Byrd, R.Grossman, A.Sleeper	
				P.Kewley, R.Usher	

3
NISO San Diego (11HQ)

The Naval Investigative Service (NIS) was created in February 1966 with three elements: a Naval Officer Director with headquarters and staff in Washington DC, NIS Offices (NISO) in US cities with major Navy and Marine Corps bases each headed by a senior Naval Officer; and NIS Resident Agencies (NISRA) as operational elements onboard USN or USMC facilities, bases, and air stations, each supervised by a senior Special Agent. One of these was NISO San Diego.

The Eleventh Naval District Intelligence Officer (DIO) in early 1966, Capt. S. Zimny, became the first Commanding Officer of NISO San Diego. He had a small staff of Navy personnel and civilians located on Fordham Street in San Diego. In a few years, the Federal Building was completed on Front Street downtown and the NISO moved into it for the next twenty or so years.

The NISO San Diego staffs changed some over the years but typically were headed by a US Navy Captain with an Executive Officer and perhaps yeomen or supply persons, an Administrative Department which was responsible for budget and finance matters, vehicles, supplies, maintenance, and communications, and an Operations Department with a Senior Special Agent designated as the Supervising Agent or later Regional Director, assistants, specialists in Technical Services and polygraph, and civilians to perform secretarial, case processing and control, and file maintenance.

Early on, civilians were not civil service employees. They were pay-grade (PG) equivalent, contract employees of the Department of the Navy. They were paid by check out of Collection and Classification of Information (C&CI) funds, written on a personal checking account of a Naval Officer. Special Agents had to keep their own record of counterintelligence and criminal cases to qualify as law enforcement agents. Toni Perrin, who was hired as a Special Agent by ONI in 1963, notes that an agent was normally hired as a PG-7, promoted to PG-9 after one year probation, and became eligible to take an examination for promotion to PG-11 after two years. Yes! An examination for promotion! Toni tells us that fifty percent of all agents had to be below PG-11. When Robert McNamara was Secretary of Defense under President John F. Kennedy, he asked why the Navy C&CI budget was so much higher than the other services. When he was told that NIS salaries were paid out of these funds, he told his people to fix it, and they did. That is how NIS personnel were converted to civil service status and Special Agents were designated as GS-1811--criminal investigators, resulting in other benefits including paid overtime and allowable unauthorized overtime (AUO) benefits. FYI, GS-11 exams for promotion continued into the 1980s.

Charles Morehead was the first of many Supervising Agents for whom Roy Mosteller worked. By the early 1960s, Bill Clayton had become Supervising Agent over the San Diego District Intelligence Office personnel. He continued to fill that position in February 1966 when NIS came into existence so he became the first Supervising Agent of NISO San Diego, assisted by Bill Poole. In the March 1968 timeframe, Bill Clayton was relieved by Earl Richey, and Clayton later transferred to the Defense Investigative Service (DIS). Assistant SA Bill Poole retired. Ted Fason and Louis Herder became Assistant Supervising Agents. A 1968 NISO San Diego roster shows NISRAs, supervisors, and numbers of assigned agents as follows:

Camp Pendleton (11PE) William Gray (12)
Long Beach (11LB) Paul Haefeli (16)
North Island (11NI) Ron Bright (5)
Port Hueneme (11PH) Roger Teel (12)
San Diego (11SD) Kenneth Seal (23)
El Toro (11ET) Jerry Wheeler (7)
MCRD (11MD) (3)
Pasadena (11PA) Charles Hurley (15)
San Bernardino (11BD) Earl Fowler (8)

The onboard total of Special Agents was 104.

Earl Richey says he was told by Jack Lynch at NIS Headquarters that his primary responsibility was to try to develop an organizational and administrative structure of the NISO San Diego agent corps. Although San Diego had one of the largest concentrations of Naval personal in the country, with few exceptions, agents worked directly from the NISO, as opposed to offices on base. Outlying field offices were few, and frequently were created based on residency of the Senior Resident Agent (SRA) rather than need. Earl Richey says he was able to create several Resident Agencies on board bases where they belonged and get capable people in charge. In 1970, Earl Richey transferred to NIS Headquarters and Sherman Bliss became Supervising Agent.

June 1971—NISO C.O. Capt. H.P.Lyon awards administrative personnel for outstanding performance

In 1972 background investigations were transferred from NIS to the newly formed Defense Investigative Service, allowing NIS to give more attention to criminal investigations and counterintelligence matters. Nearly half of NIS SAs were transferred to DIS including Bill Clayton. In September 1974, NISO San Diego manning levels were:

Chart 3-1 September 1974 NISO Manning Levels

	Allowance	On Board
Officers	4	4
Agents	77	77
Enlisted	5	5
GS	28	28
Total	114	110

By 1974, new NISRAS had been established at Naval Air Station Miramar, Naval Station San Diego, and Marine Corps Air Station Yuma, and offices had been closed in Pasadena, Los Angeles, and San Bernardino. Growth continued through the 1970s with new NISRAs at Naval Training

Center San Diego, and Marine Corps Base Twentynine Palms. NISRA San Diego was relocated to the Naval Ocean Systems Center in Point Loma. With growth came new titles: Supervising Agent became Regional Director for Operations (RDO) and Senior Resident Agent became Special Agent in Charge (SAC). In 1980, NISO San Diego was led by Capt. Burton Larkins, USN, an administrative staff of six, and an Operations Department of seven headed by RDO Greg Duffy.

In January 1981, Ted Hicks and Harry Stovall switched positions: Ted departed the NISO job of Special Assistant to the RDO (SARDO) to become NISRA Miramar ASAC and Harry left Miramar for the SARDO position. Greg Duffy was the RDO, with Deputy RDO (DRDO) Bob Brady and Assistant RDO (ARDO) Kirby Sumner. Harry's main responsibility was agent recruitment which included organizing screening boards, and new agent applicant processing. He also aided in reviewing investigative reports and participating in NISRA inspections.

Chart 3-2 January 1984 NISO Personnel

1984 NISO PERSONNEL					
	SAC	Officers	Enlisted	Agents	GS
Headquarters (HQ)		2	2	7	8
Camp Pendleton (PE)	D.Stuart	1	5	17	6
El Toro (ET)	R.Scott	0	2	7	3
Long Beach (LB)	D.Dykes	0	0	14	3
Miramar (MM)	L.Ferrell	0	0	6	2
Naval Station (ND)	D.McCoy	1	0	16	4
Naval Train. Com (NC)	V.McDonald	0	0	10	2
North Island (NI)	A.Perrin	0	0	14	3
Point Loma (11PL)	H.Abrams	1	0	12	2
Port Hueneme (11PH)	M.Embry	0	0	4	1
29 Palms (11TN)	V.McPherson	0	1	9	3
Yuma (11YU)	V.McDonald	0	0	4	1
Laboratory (11ZS)					6
Totals		5	10	120	44

In time, NISO became NIS Regional Office (NISRO). Bob Panico came to 11HQ as DRDO under Greg Duffy in July 1984, relieving Bobby Brady. ARDO was Joe Brandt then Dan McBride. Bob Helbock became ARDO from July 1984 to July 1985. During that year, Win Kuehl relieved Greg Duffy as RDO and Roger Teel was his Deputy. Helbock described his workload to include some case review, Region internal inquiries, NISRA inspections, writing annual evaluations of region SACs, and maintaining daily contact with NISHQ regarding ongoing investigations.

As SARDO from April 1985 to October 1987, Dan Simas learned that Win Kuehl had a reputation for yelling at almost anyone at anytime. Dan developed a system wherein he would call all the SACs in the region and use the phrase "Red Meat Day." This meant the RDO was looking to yell at people. When Win learned of Dan's system, he laughed and thought it funny—at least according to Dan.

1986 Management Conference Attendees

From March 1988 to December 1989, Joe Naylor served as the Western Polygraph Coordinator working out of the NISRO office on Front Street. His job was to review and oversee polygraph exams given in NCIS offices in San Diego, San Francisco, Bremerton, WA, Alaska, Japan, and the Philippines.

Steve Kahl served as the Fraud ARDO from August 1988 to April 1990 under RDOs Win Kuehl and Dennis Usrey. During his early assignment under Win Kuehl, the SARDO position was vacant and Kuehl expected Kahl to perform responsibilities of both the ARDO and SARDO positions. During this period, NIS was recruiting heavily and the SARDO was responsible for coordinating this effort at colleges throughout the Region. As such, he received and processed applications, coordinated the initial and final interview boards, and kept in touch with applicants as the processing continued. Kahl advised that 11HQ hired about eighty new SAs out of about 1500 applicants while he served as SARDO.

Another task that Steve Kahl performed was as the NIS Representative to the FBI Field Office during the CALBOMB Investigation (car bombing documented in Naval Station chapter). To monitor the joint FBI/NIS investigation including the NIS Protective Service Detail (PSD) of Capt. Rogers, by his own estimate, Kahl spent about sixteen hours/day in the FBI Command Center for about two months.

Dennis Usrey relieved Win Kuehl as RDO in December 1989. At the same time, Capt. Marty Herbst, USN, retired as NISO Commanding Officer and was not replaced by another naval officer. So Dennis Usrey became the first San Diego RDO who was, as a civilian, totally in charge of a NIS Region. Dennis recalled some of the most significant cases during his tenure as the Rogers car bombing, the visit of USSR ships to San Diego, and the Tailhook investigation— each of which is addressed elsewhere herein. Larry Ferrell served as the DRDO under Dennis Usrey from July 1989 until his retirement in Sept 1990.

As of March 1992, personnel strength in the NIS Southwest Region was as depicted:

Chart 3-3 March 1992 NISO Personnel

MARCH 1992 NISO PERSONNEL					
Office	SAC/Leader	Officer	Enlisted	Agent	Support
Headquarters	F.Melia	1	4	8	11
Camp Pendleton (PE)	V.Giame	1	4	16	7
China Lake (C	W.Taguchi	0	0	7	2
Corpus Christi (CC)	D.McBride	0	0	17	3
El Toro (ET)	M.Barrett	1	3	7	3
Forensic Laboratory	B.Armstrong	0	0	0	9
Fraud Unit L. Angeles	R.Miller	0	0	15	2
Fraud Unit San Diego	S.Kahl	0	0	14	2.5
Leps Assist Team	E.Niemela	1	6	0	3
Los Angeles	P.Anderson	0	0	17	5
Miramar (MM)	B.Smart	0	0	6	1
Mobile Train Team	J.Thurber	0	0	0	11
Naval Station (ND)	H.Stovall	1	0	18	6
North Island (NI)	W.Clookie	0	1	13	3
Polygraph Unit	P.Hurt	0	0	6	1
Port Hueneme (PH)	W.Nugent	0	0	7	2
Training Commands	J.Davies	0	0	14	3
Twentynine Palms	T.Clark	0	1	8	2
Yuma	M.Pendell	0	1	7	2
Totals		5	20	180	78

By early 1992, a very large NCIS office at Naval Station was being constructed to house the San Diego Field Office. Frank Melia, who had spent several tours in the region, came in to replace Dennis Usrey as RDO. Doug Stuart served as DRDO and John Davies reported as the Inspector General. In the next two years, the building was completed, the San Diego Field Office was established, and NISO San Diego disappeared after about twenty-eight years.

Chart 3-4 NISO San Diego

NISO SAN DIEGO									
C.O. DATES	C.O.	X.O	SA/RDO DATES	SA/RDO	ASA/DRDO	ARDO (CRIM)	ARDO (FCI)	ARDO (FRAUD)	SARDO
Feb 66-Jun 67	CAPT S.M. Zimny		Feb66-Mar68	W.Clayton	W.Poole				
Jun 67-Jun 68	W.K. Rogers		Mar68-Jun70	E.Richey	T. Fason/L.Herder				
Jun 68-Sep 68	CDR W. Vogt				T.Fason/L.Herder				
Sep 68-July 71	CAPT H.P. Lyons		Jun70-Jan73	S.Bliss	L.Herder				
Jul 71-Aug 75	CAPT C. Casserly	CDR R. Griffen	73-77	T.Nolan	P.Daly/W.Mendelson				
Aug 75-Jun 79	CAPT G. McNulty		77-80	D.Kerr		M.Nagle			
Jul 79-Sept 79	CDR W.Castellano			D.Kerr					
Oct 79-Jun 83	CAPT B. Larkins	CDR. W.Castellano	Aug80-Jul84	G. Duffy	R. Brady	K.Sumner			T. Hicks/H.Stovall
	CAPT B. Larkins	CDR J. Mahoney		G.Duffy	R.Panico	D.McBride			S.Knowles
Jun 83-Apr 86	CAPT J. Duncan	CDR J. Coughlin		G.Duffy	R.Panico	D.McBride			S.Knowles
Apr 86-Jun 86	CDR J. Coughlin		Jul84-Oct89	W.Kuehl	R.Teel	R.Helbock			S.Ferguson
Jun 86-Jun 89	CAPT M. Herbst	CDR J. Coughlin		W.Kuehl	K.Sumner	M.Bourke	J.Parkey	S.Kahl	D.Simas
			Dec89-Jan92	D.Usrey	L.Ferrell	M.Bourke	A.Sipe	S.Kahl	D.Wieland
			Jan92-Jan94	F. Melia	D.Stuart	M.Bourke	A.Sipe		D.Wieland
							B.Smart		

ADMIN SUPPORT	OTHER	
S.Smith, M.Mitsias, K.Fogelberg, B.Hannon, F.Douglas,	POLYGRAPH: T.Williams, D.Galanti, J.Pender, J.Naylor, D.Baker. P.Hurt, T.Davidson	
V.Homfeld, S. Hrencher, K.Brown, J.O'Brien, K.King, K.Smith	TECHNICAL: J.B.Greene, J.Stevens, J.Marine, P.McCreary, D.Wieland	
P.Revolinsky, D.McKinney, D.Schneiders, J.Foss, S.Harty	RECRUITING: M. Acevedo	FORENSICS: B.Nakasone

4
The Military and NIS

The presence and role of the military in NIS/NCIS was always important and at times critical. From February 1966 when NIS was created until it became NCIS in 1992, the organization was led by a senior Navy Officer. A succession of US Navy Captains or later, Rear Admirals commanded NIS through various name and operational changes until 1985 when RADM Cathal "Irish" Flynn became Commander. Thereafter, several Judge Advocate General (JAG) Corps officers commanded NIS until 1992 when the Secretary of the Navy directed reorganization of NIS, placement of the organization to report directly to the Secretary, and shifted leadership to a civilian Director, Mr. Roy D. Nedrow. There has always been a continuous military presence at NCIS Headquarters with representatives of both the US Navy and US Marine Corps filling intelligence, investigative, and supervisory positions.

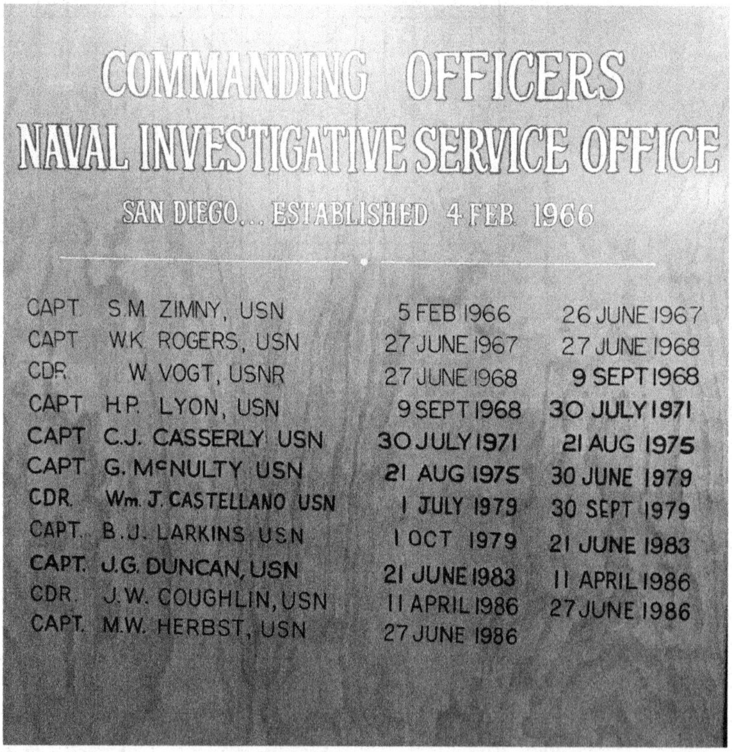

District Intelligence Officer (DIO) positions existed in the 11th Naval District as far back as 1924. Capt. S.M. Zimny was the last assigned DIO from 30 June 1965 to 6 February 1966, the date that NIS was created when he became the first Commanding Officer of NISO San Diego. Over the next twenty-three years, ten US Navy Captains or Commanders served as Commanding Officer of NISO San Diego, the last of whom was Capt. Marty Herbst, USN who was assigned until mid 1989 when he relinquished command to a civilian, Dennis Usrey. In addition to a Commanding Officer, each NISO or later NISRO had an Executive Officer, and possibly enlisted administrative personnel.

COMMANDING OFFICERS
NAVAL INVESTIGATIVE SERVICE OFFICE
SAN DIEGO... ESTABLISHED 4 FEB 1966

CAPT	S.M. ZIMNY, USN	5 FEB 1966	26 JUNE 1967
CAPT	W.K. ROGERS, USN	27 JUNE 1967	27 JUNE 1968
CDR	W. VOGT, USNR	27 JUNE 1968	9 SEPT 1968
CAPT	H.P. LYON, USN	9 SEPT 1968	30 JULY 1971
CAPT	C.J. CASSERLY USN	30 JULY 1971	21 AUG 1975
CAPT	G. McNULTY USN	21 AUG 1975	30 JUNE 1979
CDR	Wm. J. CASTELLANO USN	1 JULY 1979	30 SEPT 1979
CAPT	B.J. LARKINS USN	1 OCT 1979	21 JUNE 1983
CAPT	J.G. DUNCAN, USN	21 JUNE 1983	11 APRIL 1986
CDR	J.W. COUGHLIN, USN	11 APRIL 1986	27 JUNE 1986
CAPT	M.W. HERBST, USN	27 JUNE 1986	

NISO San Diego Commanding Officers

Military personnel have served in various roles in NIS operational offices. At one time, a NIS Representative was a Navy Officer assigned to a NISRA to perform counterintelligence duties. Such was the case with Lt John Davies in Long Beach in the mid-1960s and this writer who served as the NIS REP in Danang, Vietnam in 1971. Navy officers have been assigned to NISRAs on Navy bases as Officer Agents and enlisted people have performed admin duties. Navy enlisted investigators (9592 MOS) served in NIS offices overseas. Marine Corps officers and enlisted personnel have routinely been assigned to Marine Base NISRAs to perform both criminal and CI duties. In the 1970s and 1980s, NIS sponsored USN Reserve units whose mission was to support NISOs with a cadre of trained personnel to conduct the full range of investigative duties. In the San Diego area, personnel from two Reserve units augmented NISRAs on a routine basis. Navy Master at Arms were also part of NIS offices worldwide for many years.

Another direct connection between NIS/NCIS and the military was the active Special Agent who also served in a military reserve capacity. In the writer's memory, the following SAs were members of a USN or USMC reserve component in the San Diego region over the years while also employed by NIS/NCIS: Roy Mosteller, Bob Steele, Jack Guedalia, Bill Gray, John Davies, Carl Sundstrom, Ken Nickel, Larry Butler, Allan Sipe, Don Johnson, Paul Schubarth, Trish Hance, Don Hershberger, Bruce Smart, Dan Foley, Vic McPherson, Wes Howe, Bob Panico, Art Arrigo, and Walt Cleveland.

June 1960 L to R Bill Gray, Jack Guedalia, Art Arrigo, Warren Wade, Roy Mosteller, Bob Steele

And lastly, many more NIS Special Agents and support personnel served their country in the active military before commencing their NIS employments. Names that come to mind with a NIS tie to the San Diego Region are Mike Barrett, Robin Parks, D.J.Heintz, Leon Carroll, Steve Kahl, and Kirby Sumner. To others whom I have failed to list, I apologize for the omission and thank you for your service.

5
NISRA Port Hueneme (11PH)

John Olson, who rightfully could be called the Lord of NISRA Port Hueneme due to his lengthy service there, initially served at the Port Hueneme day office while assigned to the ONI Field Intelligence Office in Los Angeles, CA from May 1963 to Nov 1964. On November 1, 1964, John became one of the five SAs to open the 11PH office—the others being SRA Pete Ipsen, Bill Blake, Ray Rude, and Vic Coxhead. That day, according to Olson, they had a homicide to take care of at NAS Point Mugu. By 1967, 11PH had grown to twelve agents and Olson had been named ASRA. One of the new agents was John Davies who had begun his service as a Naval Officer at the ONI Field Intelligence Office in Long Beach in 1965, became a civilian Special Agent in 1967, and transferred to Port Hueneme.

The summer 1968 NISO-wide roster lists the following agents at Port Hueneme: SRA Roger Teel to replace Pete Ipsen, ASRA John Olson, Lyman Butterfield, John Davies, Don Dufur, Benjamin Hull, Jay Minor, James Stewart, Bill Tannehill, Ken Walters, Fred Wyneken, and Vic Coxhead. After Ipsen left for Japan, Olson became acting SRA (as a GS-11) until Roger Teel arrived in August 1968. Two years later, the SRA position was upgraded to GS-13 and the ASRA to GS-12. Lyman Butterfield became the ASRA. About the same time in August 1970, NAS Point Mugu—the site of the Pacific Missile Range—became a NIS Resident Unit (NISRU), and John Olson became the first Representational Resident Agent (RRA).

By mid 1971, Al Marretta had come in to replace Lyman Butterfield as ASRA, other agents had departed and 11PH had five working agents. Then Roger Teel was transferred to Camp Pendleton, two agents left NIS for the newly established Defense Investigative Service in 1972, and 11PH was left with three agents—Marretta as SRA, John Davies as ASRA, and Olson as the RRA at Point Mugu.

During his assignment at 11PH and 11MU from 1964 until his transfer to Japan in July 1973, John Olson said one highlight was his participation in a protective service detail for President Richard Nixon. Olson was replaced by Larry Ferrell who served at Point Mugu until July 1975 under SRAs Al Marretta and his relief John Stevens. After serving as ASRA for a short time under Marretta, John Davies moved to another assignment in May 1974, replaced by Mike Bourke.

In October 1979, Steve Gutshall who was the ASAC at NISRA Long Beach, was directed by NISO San Diego to proceed to NISRA Port Hueneme and relieve the SAC, John Stevens, because of a personal situation. Gutshall sat down and discussed the issue with Stevens, who was not happy with the event but agreed to make it work. Stevens proceeded to work his assignments as a professional and never complained. According to Gutshall, Stevens worked eight hours per day and stood his nighttime duty but performed very little Administrative Uncontrolled Overtime (AUO). Gutshall said he would leave Westminster on Monday, drive to 11PH, stay at the Point Mugu BOQ until Friday, and drive home Friday evening. He says it was a challenging career assignment that helped his promotion to GS-13 that year.

In about April 1980, Gutshall had completed his assignment and Charles Van Page reported in as SAC. About the same time, Kevin Edge reported in to Port Hueneme where he proceeded to serve as the RRA at Point Mugu under SACs Page, Olson, and Embry. Edge recalls the visits of President Reagan to NAS Point Mugu onboard Air Force One during which he and other agents were always part of the US Secret Service protective detail and sometimes within a few feet of the President and First Lady.

During his assignment as a GS-13 SAC of 11PH between July 1981 and January 1983, John Olson recalled assisting the US Secret Service on protective service details for President Ronald

Reagan and Vice President George H.W. Bush on about fifteen occasions. He also assisted on a protective service detail for Secretary of Defense Melvin Laird. Olson was relieved as SAC by former Honolulu police officer Mike Embry.

About one year later, Bill Nugent relieved Kevin Edge who had replaced Mike Embry. Thus, Nugent began what became nearly a ten-year assignment as SAC. It was interrupted only by a two-year assignment in Europe during which Harry Rogers came in as the 11PH SAC.

Too often, barricaded captor incidents end up in chaos, despair, and death. This story fits none of those characteristics. In mid-July 1989, John Wagner was an agent in his first year of service under SAC Harry Rogers. He had duty one weekend and was at the gym on a Saturday night when his pager activated. He called base security on a landline telephone—remember this was before cell phones—and was told there was an armed barricaded subject in base housing. Wagner attempted to call his supervisors and co-workers but was only able to connect with one other agent to respond.

In his gym clothes, Wagner headed to the residence, the perimeter of which had been secured by base police. He interviewed the subject's wife who said he was suicidal and had attempted to lock her in a bedroom with himself. Wagner called the home, the suspect we will call Joe answered, and the dialogue began. Over time, Wagner made Joe more comfortable with his questioning and understanding. It took some convincing, but finally, Joe agreed to surrender—but only to Wagner with all uniformed security out of the area. Wagner coordinated a security plan with the watch commander about the time that two other NIS agents arrived. Good timing.

Still in his gym clothes but with a pullover sweatshirt hiding his .38 cal revolver and handcuffs, GS-7 Wagner approached the residence, passing several hidden security personnel on his walk. Wagner approached Joe with his hands extended, told Joe he was unarmed, and asked Joe to show his hands and turn around. Joe complied and extended his hand to shake with Wagner. As they shook hands, Wagner applied an arm hold and got Joe to the ground and handcuffed, all the while talking to make Joe more comfortable. Joe was taken into custody without incident.

Wagner and his three officemates searched the residence where they found an arsenal of weapons in the bedroom along with boxes of ammunition.

This kind of evolution, today, involves police swat teams, command posts, surveillance aircraft, and mass media. In 1989, it involved one novice Special Agent who did everything right and ended a dangerous situation with a textbook solution. It also got Wagner a transfer to NISRA Long Beach.

The March 1992 NISO San Diego roster reflects the following personnel at 11PH: agents SAC Nugent, ASAC Bob Bryan, Ron Janson, Peter Ruggiero, and Kirk Downs and secretaries Bagasao and Burgess; and at Point Mugu, agents Y. Yoneda and Tannis Herr.

Port Hueneme became a Resident Agency of the Los Angeles Field Office in 1993 with Bill Nugent still in place as Senior Resident Agent (SRA). Rod Miller had been promoted to GM-15 SAC of the Field Office and Ron Benefeld and Russ Porter were the ASACs.

In July 1995, Wagner returned to the Port Hueneme office which was unchanged other than some personnel. Bob Bryan served as the SRA relieved later by Marilyn Hourican. John Wagner had been promoted to the GS-12 level, still working general criminal investigations. Wagner remembers the good narcotics work on the central coast, specifically two operations he managed at two Seabee Battalions. In both ops, he used Cooperating Witnesses in proactive reverse sting settings—posing to sell narcotics or dangerous drugs to sailors without entrapment. In one op, Wagner said agents arrested twelve "buyers" and in the other op, fourteen subjects were arrested.

There must be something to like about the Port Hueneme office and the California central coast. Few other NISRAs known to this writer have as many "long term" employees as this one. John Olson, John Davies, Bill Tannehill, Kevin Edge, John Stevens, and Bill Nugent each appear to have spent upwards of five years at this paradise. At least two of these men, in addition to Lyman Butterfield, retired in the area.

Chart 5-1 NISRA Port Hueneme

NISRA PORT HUENEME (11PH)				
	SRA/SAC	ASRA/ASAC	OTHER AGENTS	ADMIN
Nov64-Aug68	N.P. Ipsen		R.Rude, W. Blake, V.Coxhead, J.Olson	
		J.V. Olson	J.Minor, L.Butterfield, D.Dufer, B.Hull,	
			J.Stewart, F.Wyneken, B.Middleton,	
			W.Tannehill, K.Walters, J.Davies	
Aug68--Oct72	R. Teel	J.V. Olson	J.Davies, W.Tannehill, B.Hull, J.Stewart,	
		L.Butterfield	J.V.Olson (MU), K.Walters, V.Coxhead	
		A.Marretta	D.Dufer, J.Minor, F.Wyneken	
Oct 72-Jun75	A.Marretta	J.Davies	J.Olson (MU),W.Tannehill, D.Dufer	B.Slate
			L.Ferrell (MU), M.Bourke	
Jun75-Oct79	J.Stevens		L.Ferrell (MU), M.Bourke, W.Wittenberger	
Oct79-Apr80	S. Gutshall		J.Stevens, W.Wittenberger (MU), K.Edge,	Beverly (LNU)
Apr80-Jul81	C.V. Page		R.K. Edge (MU), J.Stevens	
Jul81-Jan 83	J.Olson	R.K.Edge	R.K. Edge (MU), K.Larson, A.Doty, J.Stevens	
Jan 83-unk	R.M. Embry		R.K. Edge (MU), J.Stevens, E.Kunigonis,	R.Bagasao
unk-Jul84	R.K. Edge			
Jul 84-Apr86	W.Nugent	G.Jacobs	J.D'Maggio (MU), P.Ruggiero, D.Winslow,	
			J. Spinosa, M.Gauoette, R.Janson	
Apr86-Jul88	H.Rogers	G.Jacobs	J.Wagner, K.Downs, D.Winslow, L.Wolfe,	R.Bagasao,
		R.Bryan	B.Bryan, P.Ruggiero, R.Janson	J.Coffey
Jul 88-Apr94	W.Nugent	R.Bryan-FCI	R.Janson, P.Ruggiero, K.Downs (FCI)	R.Bagasao,
			Y.Yoneda (MU), T.Herr (MU)-FCI, C.O'Gara	M.Burgess
Became Resident Agency of the Los Angeles Field Office in 1993				
95--96	SRA-B.Bryan		J.Reed (MU), D.Clayton (FCI),	M.Burgess
	M.Hourican		J.Wagner, C.Ogara, T. McLaughlin-crim	

6
NISRA China Lake (11CK)

Ridgecrest, CA, is a small city on Highway 395 about 145 miles north of San Bernardino. It became incorporated in 1963, at which time its population was about 6,000. Ridgecrest was and still is the home of the Naval Air Weapons Station, China Lake. In July 1965, Marv Frankel was the first Special Agent assigned to a one-man office at China Lake which came under NISRA San Bernardino. For the next two years, Marv commuted back and forth between China Lake and San Bernardino where his family lived. Marv then obtained housing on base and moved his wife and two young daughters to China Lake. In 1969, Marv was relieved of his duties by Steve Kaupp and moved with his family to NISRA Philippines.

By 1972, 11CK remained a NIS Resident Unit, but supported by NISRA San Diego. Paul Clark filled the NISRU position in the 1973 to1975 timeframe. NISRA Twentynine Palms started up in 1975 and put Frank Traser at 11CK followed in June 1977 by Harry Reeves who spent five years there. As of August 1982, 11CK with RRA John Hopeck was under the auspices of NISRA Twentynine Palms and SAC Steve Gutshal.

In August 1984, 11CK was elevated to NISRA status with John Hopeck becoming SAC. He departed China Lake in July 1987, and his successor, Al Hughes, reported in December 1987.

While GM-13 SAC at 11CK, Al Hughes said his office performed the gamut of investigative activities. In summary, he said their work included: a significant alleged espionage investigation involving a covert surveillance operation in the European theater without host country knowledge; initiated and supported double agent operations; established a joint criminal operations task force with local city and county law enforcement agencies resulting in the recovery of over one million dollars in stolen government property and illegal drugs; initiated successful fraud investigations involving contracts exceeding fifty-one million dollars; and directing the arrests of over one hundred perpetrators of various crimes who were convicted of felonies in state and federal courts.

Wendell Taguchi, who began his NIS career in the San Diego Region in 1974, ended it as well as the last SAC of China Lake. Tag relieved Al Hughes in late 1991 and stayed in place until January 1997 when he retired. He particularly recalls the great group of agents in place when he assumed the SAC position and the super relationships they cultivated with the local police and county sheriff deputies with whom they conducted many joint counter-narcotics operations.

Chart 6-1 NISRA China Lake

CHINA LAKE (11CK)				
65-69	M.Frankel		assigned from NISRA San Bernardino	
70-73	S.Kaupp		assigned from NISRA San Bernardino	
73-75	P.Clark		assigned from NISRA San Diego	
75-Jun 77	R.Traser		assigned from NISRA 29 Palms	
Jun 77-Aug 82	H.Reeves		assigned from NISRA 29 Palms	
Aug 82-Aug 84	J.Hopeck	D.Reppard	assigned from NISRA 29 Palms	
Office became NISRA China Lake in August 1984				
	SAC	ASAC	OTHER AGENTS	ADMIN
Aug 84-Jul 87	J.Hopeck	A.Booth	C.Hatch	
Dec 87-Dec 91	A.Hughes	A. Booth	R.Hedenskog, D.Cannon, D. Truesdale	
			R.Barbian, C.Hatch, K.Minick, T.Herr	
Nov 91-Jan 97	W.Taguchi	A.Booth	D.Truesdale, K.Minnick, P.Bradney, R.Baer	P.Rousakis,
			G.Mayer-FCI, C.Rosenlund, Diane (LNU),	L.Rogers
Office became part of Los Angeles Field Office in July 1993				

7
NISRA Pasadena (11PA)/NISRA Los Angeles (11LA)

Ted Miller began his long NIS career as a GS-7 contract employee at NISRA Pasadena in March 1967 and remained there until mid-1968. The office was located on Green St. as described in a following paragraph. Ted said his first SRA was Bill Tannehill who had become such in 1966. Tannehill was relieved by Chuck Hurley in the fall of 1967. Gail Wilkes was the ASRA. Miller said the Pasadena office covered all of Los Angeles County outside of the City of Los Angeles, and it was common for Miller to have to drive to the San Fernando Valley or Compton or Ontario to accomplish leads on background investigations. In the fall of 1968, Art Arrigo arrived, relieved Hurley as SRA for a short time, and transferred on to Alameda where he retired.

In the summer to fall period of 1968, Hurley moved over to west Los Angeles and opened NISRA Los Angeles as its first SRA. Miller was named ASRA along with Jim Scanlan, other street agents, and support personnel. The office was located in a VA hospital at 11000 Wilshire Blvd. near UCLA. Miller recalls the office conducted mainly background investigations in the City of Los Angeles.

NISRA Pasadena 1967/68

Dan Foley became SRA of NISRA Pasadena in January 1969, following Gail Wilkes who had temporarily filled the SRA position after Arrigo departed for NISRA Alameda in late 1968. At that time, the NISRA occupied the second floor of a building at 1030 E. Green St., Pasadena, an old historical building at the intersection of Colorado Blvd. and Lake Blvd. The first floor, according to

Foley, was occupied by the Office of Naval Research. He elaborated that there were showroom glass windows on either side of the main entrance and a circular staircase with a wall mural leading to the second floor. Foley said that personnel mainly used a side street entrance to come and go. He added that it was reported in a historical article in the local press that the building was once a brothel. Foley said his office area of responsibility was all of Los Angeles County less the city of Los Angeles. The 11PA workload consisted mainly of background investigations and leads from other NIS offices, as the county is home to a significant number of DOD contractors.

In about 1970, NISHQ directed 11PA to apprehend two active duty enlisted marines who were flaunting their deserter status as Vietnam War protesters in President Nixon's hometown of Whittier, CA. The marines were living with a group of people in the basement of the Quaker Church in Whittier. The NISRA coordinated the matter with the US Attorney's office in Los Angeles and the Whittier Police Department. According to Dan Foley, the NIS agents arrived at the church at the crack of dawn with only boot camp photos of the marines, their service weapons and flashlights. They found the front doors unlocked and proceeded to the basement. There, they discovered many dirty, smelly men and women sprawled out on the floor in sleeping bags and mattresses. They identified themselves and began sorting through the occupants looking for the two marines. The NIS agents found two suspects and took them upstairs where they realized that one of the men was not one of the deserters. They took him back to the basement and found the correct deserter marine. They quickly loaded the two marines into separate NIS vehicles and got away from the church without contact with any church officials or the press. They proceeded to the Provost Marshal's Office at Camp Pendleton where the two deserters were released to military control.

In June 1970, Ted Hicks was hired by NIS and sent as a new GS-9 to NISRA Los Angeles where Chuck Hurley was in place as SRA and ninetyfive percent of the office work was BIs. In his time there, Hicks recalls many of the Pasadena agents—Beauchamp, Sheldon, Dunn—relocated to the 11LA office. As NIS was preparing for the creation of the Defense Investigative Service (DIS), which would result in the loss of a large number of billets, many agents were told they would be RIF'ed or terminated from NIS and forced to employ with DIS or elsewhere. Hicks decided his best option was to volunteer to serve NIS in Vietnam where he transferred in the summer of 1971.

With the establishment of DIS in early 1972, NISRA Pasadena was merged into NISRA Los Angeles, then still supervised by Chuck Hurley. Dan Foley was the last SRA of 11PA, departing in December 1971.

Chart 7-1 NISRA Pasadena

NISRA PASADENA (11PA)				
	SRA	ASRA	OTHER AGENTS	ADMIN
unk-mid67	W.Tannehill	G.Wilkes	R.Beauchamp, J.Cox, R.Hogge, D.Goodwillie	
			S.Kaupp, T.Miller, D.Neuman, J.Scanlan,	
			D.Sheldon, R.Valentine, F.Fisher, J.Dunn	
mid67-68	C.Hurley	G.Wilkes	R.Beauchamp, J.Cox, R.Hogge, D.Goodwillie	L.Rackley
			S.Kaupp, T.Miller, D.Neuman, J.Scanlan,	
			D.Sheldon, R.Valentine, F.Fisher, J.Dunn	
68	A.Arrigo	G.Wilkes	R.Beauchamp, D.Goodwillie, J.Dunn	
68-Jan69	G.Wilkes			
Jan 69-Dec 71	D.Foley	G.Wilkes/	D.Goodwillie, G.Hall, K.Walters, G.Clark	M.Baca,
		R.Beauchamp	J.Ferranato, D.Strahan, W.Boggs, J.Dunn	S.Jeffs
			F.Orrantia, D.Peyovich,	
With establishment of DIS in early 1972, 11PA merged into NISRA Los Angeles				

8
NISRAS Pomona/San Bernardino/Twentynine Palms (11PM/BD/TN)

In 1966, Earl Fowler came west from NIS Headquarters to replace Bill Tannehill as SRA of NISRA Pomona which was located in the US Navy Reserve Building. Tannehill was transferred to the SRA position in Pasadena. The plan, according to Earl Fowler, was to relocate the Pomona office to San Bernardino or Riverside and to establish one-man offices (called resident units) at Marine Corps Base Twentynine Palms and Marine Corps Supply Center Barstow. At that time, a resident unit already existed at Naval Weapons Center China Lake. Other agents assigned were Bob Curtis, Fred Beattie, and Jack Dunn at Pomona and Marv Frankel at China Lake.

In early 1967, Fowler moved the NISRA to Norton Air Force Base in Riverside. The office was temporarily located in a World War II vintage building until space became available in the US Air Force Office of Special Investigations (OSI) Regional Headquarters building. The NISRA hired two secretaries but lost agents Curtis and Dunn to transfer. Shortly, Fowler established resident units at Twentynine Palms with Ray Rude assigned and at Barstow with Rex Morris in place. According to Earl Fowler, both of these men faced some obstacles with some members of the commands they supported but overcame the issues through their excellent liaison abilities. The area of responsibility for NISRA San Bernardino was San Bernardino County and Clark County, Nevada, which included Las Vegas and Sandia Base.

In June or July 1968, Bob Panico transferred from NISRA Long Beach to NISRA San Bernardino in the newly established billet of ASRA. In the next few months, new hire agents Jack Cox, Frank Orrantia, and James Wilson arrived and Beattie and Frankel departed. Steve Kaupp came in to replace Frankel at China Lake. George McClellan came from Pasadena and Orrantia departed for Vietnam.

Bob Panico's comment about this assignment, "Hot!!!" He recalled working a case at Twentynine Palms with Ray Rude with the temperature at 120 degrees and a popsicle melted before you could eat it.

In July 1970, Earl Fowler PCS'd to Hawaii and Panico became acting SRA for a short time until he was ordered to transfer to NISRA Okinawa as SRA. Paul Clark came in as SRA and is thought to have stayed in that position until the NISRA was disestablished in late 1971 or early 1972 due to the establishment of the Defense Investigative Service (DIS). Paul Clark is believed to have transferred to China Lake after 11BD was disestablished. In August 1971, Henry Lingan

NISRA San Bernardino

replaced Ray Rude at Twentynine Palms. By 1972, NIS Resident Units (NISRU) at Barstow, China Lake, and Twentynine Palms all were brought under the purview of NISRA San Diego.

In July 1972, Roy Mosteller became the SRA of NISRA San Diego. Henry Lingan was in place as the RRA at Twentynine Palms, Paul Clark at China Lake, and Vern McDonald had moved into the Barstow RRA. Lingan recalls that he had a one-room office next to the Legal Office and Base Commander's Office. He said he always had a heavy caseload and dictated his reports to be sent to San Diego for typing. In July 1974, Lingan left for Rota, Spain to be replaced by Larry Skinner, assisted by Bob L'Heureux. In time, Jim Antink relieved McDonald in Barstow. All offices continued to report to the SRA in San Diego.

A NISO San Diego personnel roster dated February 1975 shows the Twentynine Palms and Barstow installations still served by NISRA San Diego. Therefore, this writer believes that NISRA Twentynine Palms was likely established in the summer of 1977 with Al Deahl as the first SRA following his transfer from NISRA Miramar. He was assisted by Stan White followed by Mike Wolfe.

Jerry Nance reported aboard 11TN in July 1979 and was immediately dispatched by SRA Deahl to Barstow to relieve Tom Liehr. Sometime later, one of Jerry's informants reported that an employee at the repair division stole two Jeeps from the facility the night before. Personally owned vehicles were not allowed in the fenced area which was guarded 24/7 by Marine MPs. The employee showed up with a large rental truck, told the guard he had been kicked out by his wife, and said the truck was to move his stuff after shift. Instead, he and a buddy drove two jeeps up into the truck and left after thanking the guard for allowing him to park on the base. Jerry surveilled the suspect's residence and got photographs of the suspect working on the jeeps and moving around engine blocks, transmissions and other heavy car parts. This was interesting since the suspect was on ninety days of sick leave for a job related injury as he hurt his back.

Jerry obtained a federal search warrant and seized the jeeps but one problem came up right away. He could not prove that the jeeps were government property. When jeeps came in for repair, they were parked in a line awaiting inspection. If the jeep was deemed repairable, it went into another line, fixed, inspected, and returned to duty. However, legally it was not considered government property while it was in this process until it passed inspection. If thought not repairable, it was sent to be destroyed.

In July 1982, Jerry Nance was relieved by Bob Bernasconi who was to become a legend as he remained in place in Barstow for at least the next fifteen years. Shortly after Jerry departed, Mark Andrews reported in as the second agent at Barstow.

Steve Gutshall, who served as the SAC of 11TN from August 1980 to August 1983, recalls the following cases from his days at 11TN: Some marines assigned to the MCB Communications Center got lazy and, rather than destroying classified material in accordance with proper procedures, they buried several bags in the desert. Once identified, they took NIS agents to the location and dug up several bags of confidential and secret material to include some special category NIS material.

In another case, NIS identified two marines graduating from Military Police training and recruited them to operate under cover to purchase drugs. After arrival on base and acting as regular marines, they identified and purchased drugs from about twenty marines assigned to MCB Twenty-nine Palms.

Ron Janson came to 11TN as ASAC from NISRA Camp Lejeune in August 1982 as Gutshall was completing his second year as SAC. His predecessor, Mike Wolfe, had previously departed. Janson was still in place when Vic McPherson relieved Gutshall as SAC in mid-

1983. McPherson served in this position until June 1986 when he turned the office over to Mike Embry. Vic recalls that his office supervised NISRU Barstow the entire time he was SRA and supervised NISRU China Lake until it became a NISRA in 1984.

One of the most significant cases in the history of NIS is known as Tailhook. The primary lead office in this case was NISRA Twentynine Palms whose area of responsibility included Clark County, NV. The initial investigation centered on the Las Vegas Hilton Hotel, site of the 1991 Tailhook Convention. The following is furnished by Tom Clark who was assigned as SAC of 11TN during the entire duration of the Tailhook investigation. After the case received national media attention, the number of "victims" increased, most of the Las Vegas leads were completed, and the scope of the inquiry ballooned with leads to NIS offices covering all Navy and Marine Corps Air Stations. One lead sent to 11TN had a dramatic effect on the NIS.

The lead was to interview an aviator assigned to Twentynine Palms who was thought to have information concerning a hospitality suite where some assaults had reportedly occurred. While trying to convince SA Clark that none of his friends could have been involved, the officer casually mentioned that the Secretary of the Navy, H. Lawrence Garrett, had been in that suite. Clark documented this information and the control office included it in subsequent reporting. When the media realized this info, it accused the Navy of a coverup. When the dust settled, the Navy had a new Secretary, NIS had a new name—NCIS, and a new civilian Director ordered to report directly to the Secretary.

Chart 8-1 NISRA Pomona/San Bernardino

NISRA POMONA/SAN BERNARDINO (11BD)				
	SRA/SAC	ASRA/ASAC	OTHER AGENTS	ADMIN
unk-66	W.Tannehill		R.Curtis, F.Beattie, J.Dunn, M.Frankel (CK)	
66--July 70	E.Fowler	B.Panico	J.Cox, J.Wilson, F.Orrantia, J.Dunn	L.Palazolla,
			R.Morris (BA), R.Rude(TN), M.Frankel (CK)	S. Salvini
Jul70-Sep70	B.Panico		same	
Sep70-late71	Paul Clark		S.Kaupp (CK), R.Morris BA), R.Rude (TN),	L.Palazolla,
			G.McClellan, J.Cox, F.Orrantia, J.Wilson	S. Salvini

Chart 8-2 NISRA Twentynine Palms

NISRA TWENTYNINE PALMS (11TN)				
	RRA-29 Palms	RRA-Barstow	AGENTS	ADMIN
67-Aug71	R. Rude	R.Morris	assigned from NISRA San Bernardino	
Aug71-Jul74	H.Lingan	V.McDonaldJ.Antink	assigned from NISRA San Diego	
Jul74-75	L.Skinner/	J.Antnk	assigned from NISRA San Diego	
	R.L'Heureux			
	SRA/SAC	ASRA/ASAC		
75-Aug80	A.Deahl	S.White-M.Wolfe	T.Liehr (BW), G.Nance (BW), H.Reeves (CK)	F.Gibson
Aug80-Aug83	S.Gutshall	M.Wolfe-R.Janson	G.Nance (BW), J.Andrews (BW)	G.Crawford
			H.Reeves (CK),D.Reppard (CK),	F.Gibson
			R.Bernasconi (BW), J.Hopeck (CK)	
			G.Jacobs, D.Johnson, J.Harrington	
			C.Reno, D.Shunck, D.Dunkleburger (USMC)	
Mar83-Jun86	V.H.McPherson	R.Janson, G.Witte	J.Hopeck (CK, A.Booth (CK)	F.Gibson.
			J.Harrington, D.Johnson, D.Thornhill,	V.Marshall
			P.Chavez, F.Bledsoe, S.James	
Jun86-Jun89	M.Embry	G.Witte	R.Bernasconi (BW), B.Call (FCI)	
Jun89-Jul93	T.Clark	G.Witte, L.Lockard,	D.Smith, D.Hertberg, T.Moses,	F.Gibson,
			B.Iorio, P.Garza, D.Schuck	
Office became subordinate to Los Angeles Field Office				
Jul93-Jan97	T.Clark	L.Lockard, B.Call		
Jan97-	K.Marks			

9
NISRA Long Beach/Los Angeles (11LB)

By the time the Korean War began in 1950, Roy Mosteller had graduated from college and was self employed in Long Beach as a Public Accountant. He had served in the US Navy as a Yeoman during World War II and had later joined the Naval Reserve. He wrote a letter to the Director of Naval Intelligence recapping his WWII service in telecommunications censorship and applied for return to active duty. Within a very short time, Mosteller found himself on active duty as a Yeoman First Class assigned to the District Intelligence Office (DIO) San Diego. After a two-year assignment during which he became acquainted with several of the Special Agents (SA) employed in the DIO, Mosteller volunteered to extend his active service for one year in return for permission to work as an agent himself. His offer was accepted and Mosteller was posted to the Field Intelligence Office, Long Beach, a subordinate unit of the DIO San Diego where he conducted background investigations (BI) with three experienced agents and lived at his family home.

Mosteller had a full caseload of BIs but very much enjoyed his occasional involvement in a criminal investigation being conducted by one of the experienced agents. At the end of his one-year Yeoman/civilian assignment, Mosteller applied for a position as a civilian Special Agent and was hired as such in November 1953.

Throughout the 1950s and early 1960s, investigative work in the greater Los Angeles area was performed by Special Agents of the Field Intelligence Office, Los Angeles, CA, another subordinate unit of the DIO San Diego. Early on, there were three agents in the Long Beach Office that Mosteller joined, six others in the main Los Angeles office, and a few in the Pasadena office. John Olson, who is prominent in the history of the Port Hueneme office, began his career in May 1963 at the Los Angeles ONI office.

PLANK OWNER

To all Sailors wherever ye may be: and to all SALTS, SEA LAWYERS, SWABS, LAND LUBBERS, SQUARE-KNOT ADMIRALS, GUN DECKERS, AND ALL THE OTHER ASSORTED SCAVENGERS OF THE SEVEN SEAS Greetings:

AND BE IT KNOWN: By all ye earthly mortals and others who may be distinguished and honored by his presence That

John G. Davies

WAS AN HONORED MEMBER OF THE FIRST AND THE MOST ILLUSTRIOUS CREW WHICH DISTINGUISHED ITSELF FOREVER WHEN IT Commissioned the U.S. Naval Investigative Service Office, San Diego And, for this Good AND SUFFICIENT REASON, HE IS ENTITLED BY THE LAWS OF THE SEA, TO ALL THE RIGHTS AND PRIVILEGES OF A PLANK OWNER

BE IT FURTHER UNDERSTOOD: That he is entitled also to a clear, free, open and unencumbered title to a single plank in the deck of the aforementioned illustrious until THIS FINAL, ACCURATE SELECTION WILL BE MADE IN ORDER OF SENIORITY according to the treasured, honorable records contained in Davey Jones' Log Book DISOBEY THESE ORDERS UNDER EXTREME PENALTY OF MY DISPLEASURE

Commissioned 4 February 1966

Plank Owner certificate John Davies

John Davies was an active duty Navy Ltjg assigned to the Field Intelligence Office, Long Beach from February 1965 to March 1967. His first SRA was Jack Guedalia who went on to a long and distinguished NIS career. On February 4, 1966—the day NIS was created—John gained a new title, NISO Representative, and a certificate from the DIO as a Plank Owner of NIS. Nearly a year later, John was hired as a civilian Special Agent.

In June 1966, Bob Panico transferred from NIS Headquarters to NISRA Long Beach, then one of the two largest Navy installations on the West Coast. The SRA at the time was Art Arrigo who transferred to Los Angeles and was temporarily replaced by Chuck Hurley and then by Paul Haefeli who came west from NIS Headquarters. The ASRA during this timeframe was Dick Childs. The NIS office was located in a Federal Building at the intersection of Long Beach Boulevard and Third Street. This building also housed the FBI and the main Long Beach Post Office. Circa 1967, the NISRA moved to the new customs building on Terminal Island.

Bob Panico recalled the following about a very large commissary located off base where significant thefts were occurring. He says many hours were spent on surveillances to catch the suspects who were believed to be employees. Someone recommended putting guard dogs inside the building when it was closed. The dogs ate the meat in the meat department!

Bob also remembered more about the early days in Long Beach. Terminal Island was the home of a large naval base, large shipyard, and large supply center. According to Bob, one had to go across a shaky pontoon bridge to reach Terminal Island. On the mainland side of the bridge was a landmark amusement park, the Long Beach Pike, which was always populated with sailors and plenty of available narcotics. Bob says that many hours were spent at the Pike on surveillance operations with the Long Beach Police Department.

Bob Panico transferred to NISRA San Bernardino in June 1968. In July, a NISO San Diego roster showed the following at 11LB: SRA Paul Haefeli, Robert Aiken, William Andre, James Antink, James Bouchard, Dick Childs, Fred Ghio, Dennis Hamilton, Bill Hengler, Alan Jarvis, Edwin Koller, Harold Kurkjian, George Meglemre, Robert Mutch, Don Roberts, and Allen Wilk.

Dick Childs came to 11LB in January 1967, his orders designating him as the Principal Assistant to the SRA who was Art Arrigo, followed by Chuck Hurley and Paul Haefeli. On October 16, 1967, Childs was officially designated the ASRA, a position in which he served until his departure in January 1969

The February 1975 NISO Roster shows Matt Hudgins as the 11LB SRA, Phil Curley as ASRA, Jeff Arnold, Henry Bister, Al Keller, Hugh Kimbell, Hugh Ward, David Watson, and John Eversoll as other agents, and Janet Dubois and Nancy Gomez as admin personnel.

Steve Gutshall reported in to the Long Beach NISRA in September 1979 as the ASRA or ASAC. According to Steve, Ron Salmon transferred from NIS Headquarters to the SAC position at Long Beach in late 1978 or early 1979. Of the eight 11LB street agents, four were new hires. He recalls that the workload was ten to fifteen cases per agent, mostly various crimes against property (Cat 6) and crimes against persons (Cat 7). None were remarkable. In October 1979, the NISO San Diego Assistant Regional Director of Operations, Bob Brady, told Gutshall that he was being sent temporarily to NISRA Port Hueneme (11PH) to relieve the then current SAC John Stevens. Gutshall returned to Long Beach after the temporary 11PH assignment.

As of January 1984, NISRA Long Beach was staffed by SAC David Dykes, ASAC Jeff Arnold, K.D. Armfield, Duane Bradley, Leon Carroll, David Depriest, M.S.Forner, Marv Frankel, Paul Graf, Don Hendrick, M.P. Kishman, C.D. Olson, D.L.Perritt, and Susan Volpe. Charles Moss was serving as RRA at the Regional Medical Center, and the admin persons were Janet Skelton, C.Sheehan, and D.Candanoza.

Rick Warmack, who was assigned to 11LB from July 1984 as a brand new GS-7 to December

1989 as a GS-12, recalled a bomb investigation. Rick arrived for work at around half past seven one morning and was told by the SAC, Chuck Bickley, that he had gotten a call from the USS Peleliu Commanding Officer who reported that his Executive Officer (XO) had discovered a pipe bomb under his vehicle. Rick was told to go to an address approximately three miles from the Long Beach Naval Station. The XO had gone for his morning run along the beach and returned, entering his building through the parking garage. As he passed his car, he saw a suspicious string taped to the side of the driver's side door with duct tape. The string disappeared under the car. Wondering what it was and a bit irritated that someone had taped it to his car, he pulled the string and it had a 3x5 index card attached to it. Now even more curious, he got down and looked under the car and saw what was obviously a pipe bomb taped to the undercarriage. He then realized he should not have pulled the string and immediately went in and called 911.

When Rick arrived on scene, the Long Beach Police Department had evacuated the area and cordoned off almost a block. The Los Angeles County Sheriff's Office Bomb Squad was also on scene. Rick got enough detail from the Police and the XO to realize that NIS needed to begin investigation on the ship as the XO virtually had no life outside his job nor did he have anyone he would suspect in the local community. Rick also was able to speak to the Bomb Squad Officer in Charge and discovered that they had transported the bomb to the beach and rendered it safe. He also told Rick that this was a viable explosive device, so Rick knew there was a serious situation and not just a prank intended to scare the XO.

Rick returned to the Naval Station NIS office where he and other agents began planning screening interviews of almost three thousand sailors assigned onboard the ship. He recalls taking about fifteen agents to the ship, setting up locations for interviews, coordinating with the Command, and interviewing each person. By eleven in the morning, they had discovered two things; the XO was universally hated as he was known to issue harsh penalties under his Non-Judicial punishment authority, and he had recently issued such harsh sentences to a handful of sailors. A while later, they had identified these "potential" suspects and began interrogating them, with one exception. One of them had not reported for work and could not be reached. Rick and another Agent were assigned to find him. Quickly, they discovered that this sailor was an unauthorized absentee and had spent the night with his girlfriend. They found her and during interview, she said that the sailor had been very upset and was acting in an erratic manner. She provided possible locations where he may be and finally, Rick was able to contact him and convince him to come in to the Naval Station. Once there, he was interrogated and quickly admitted to placing the bomb under the XO's car but claimed it was only meant to scare him and that he (the sailor) knew it would not work.

Rick recalls working for months with the LASO Bomb Squad, as NIS knew the subject's defense would be that it was not a functional explosive device and only meant to scare the XO since he was such a "tyrant." In the end, the suspect was convicted because of the efforts of the entire Long Beach NCISRA and the LASO Bomb Squad.

When asked about his memories of this five-year assignment, Rick acknowledged that Long Beach had a personality of its own. He said that his office always had a strong feeling of camaraderie and teamwork that carried into each of their personal lives. They worked hard and played hard, with lots of happy hour get-togethers on Fridays, promotion parties at the O Club, and even some weekend personal parties. When he started in 1984, there were ten GS-07 Special Agents in the office and this obviously led to a lot of learning on-the-job. Some of them were former cops who were able to adjust faster while others were not and needed more guidance. All needed help with learning the NIS report writing. When he as a new agent needed help, Rick said he found it, not only from his fellow GS-07s, but mostly from more senior agents.

Rick also remembers that this was not a choice assignment for married agents. The cost of living in California was high and people always looked to transfer to more cost-friendly offices such as in Florida, North Carolina, South Carolina and overseas. The issue was compounded because no one wanted to come to California so "escaping" was difficult. Rick related he was single and fine with staying in Long Beach as he enjoyed the work, the camaraderie, the social life, and the weather. Due to the strong desire of agents wanting to transfer, Rick vividly recalls the rush to the teletype machine when agents came to work during transfer season to see who might be lucky enough to be transferred.

After a year or so on the job, Rick began working drug operations. Most nights, office agents would be doing surveillance, a drug buy, or a drug bust. When the narcotics agents would ask around the office for help, they always found it. He remembers a lot of drug operations worked with the Long Beach Police Department in some undesirable areas of Long Beach. Deterrent "buy/bust" operations were the most fun. The Police would identify areas where open drug trade occurred and where NIS intelligence indicated Navy personnel were buying their drugs. NIS would dress an agent in a Navy uniform and send him into the streets in a van to buy drugs. When surveillance showed a drug buy had occurred, NIS agents and Police would make a very obvious and public arrest. Many of these involved chasing suspects through alleys, between houses, over fences, and into the streets. After several of these operations in known drug areas, a sailor couldn't buy drugs if he waived a $100 bill out the window according to Warmack.

Special Agent Mark D. Ridley joined the NIS in 1987, serving in NISRA Long Beach. Ridley was working in Special Operations in September 1989 when John Wagner reported onboard, and as a Special Agent Afloat aboard the USS FORRESTAL in 1990. Wagner recalled the great crew of individuals in 11LB whose caseloads included high quality narcotics cases, government property thefts, and homicides. Wagner said that the office worked through the Los Angeles riots which involved some sailors who looted liquor from a Long Beach liquor store. He recalled that agents worked out an agreement with the Los Angeles District Attorney's Office which allowed NIS to obtain and serve search warrants in the county. Wagner pointed out that several of the 11LB agents rose to senior leadership positions in NIS/NCIS in later years—Ridley to Deputy Director, Mark Clayton to the NCIS Inspector General, Greg Bachman and Leon Carroll to GM-15 SAC, and Sheldon Beddo to ASAC. Wagner neglected to include himself as he ultimately became a Senior Executive Service (SES) manager in NCIS.

In the early 1990s, Pete Anderson was the GM-14 SAC of 11LB. In 1991, the Base Realignment and Closure Commission (BRAC) directed the thirty-eight ships and 17,000 personnel assigned to the Naval Base be moved to other west coast bases. In 1992, the NISRA downsized and changed its name to NISRA Los Angeles.

As of March 1992, the NIS Southwest Region personnel listing reflected the following assigned to NISRA Los Angeles: SAC Pete Anderson, Crim ASAC Charles Moss, FCI ASAC Paul Valentine, T. Donnelly, D. Daly, D. Lauver, A. Burghard, M. Relyea, R. Mebs, D. Hausman, D. Otterbacher, D. Nelson, J. Wagner, D. See, S. Brady, S. Beddo, and D. Watson. Admin personnel were D.Moore, V.Otterbacher, T.Onorato, and D.Balk

In 1993, NCISRA Los Angeles relocated to Upland with mainly a fraud investigation mission. Anderson moved to the Upland area in the summer of 1993 where he remained until his retirement in October 1993. He was relieved as SAC by Rod Miller. Anderson's Crim ASAC, Charles Moss, remained Resident Agent in charge (RAC) of NCISRA Long Beach which relocated to Seal Beach. The Upland office became the Los Angeles Field Office which brought in seven NCIS offices under the single SAC, Rod Miller.

Pete Anderson recalled one specific criminal matter which stands out because of the manner in which it was pursued. SA John Wagner and others needed to check on a suspect in a light industrial area where a conventional surveillance operation could easily be compromised. So they requested and received permission to use the Goodyear blimp which was based nearby as an aerial surveillance platform. It worked, they worked, and the bad guys didn't like the result.

The Los Angeles Field Office management structure in March 1994 consisted of SAC Miller, ASAC Michael Barrett, ASAC Fraud Russ Porter, LAFO FCI Paul Valentine, China Lake RAC Wendell Taguchi, El Toro RAC Ken Oglesbee, Long Beach RAC Charles Moss, Port Hueneme RAC Bill Nugent; and Twentynine Palms RAC Tom Clark.

Chart 9-1 NISRA Long Beach

NISRA LONG BEACH				
	SRA/SAC	ASRA/ASAC	OTHER AGENTS	ADMIN
65-mid66	J.Guedalia		R.Maloof, S.Chenowith, J.Burns, A.Jarvis	
			H.Kurkjian, Ltjg J.Davies	
mid66-Jan67	A.Arrigo	R.Childs	B.Panico, S.Chenowith, J.Burns, R.Hanson, A.Jarvis,	3 secs
			J.Antink, H.Kurkjian, D.Hamilton, J.Nester, R.Ryan,	
			W.Hengler, C.Ervin, W.Andre, F.Ghio, Ltjg J.Davies	
Jan67-mid67	C.Hurley	R.Childs	B.Panico, S.Chenowith, J.Burns, R.Hanson, A.Jarvis,	
			J.Antink, H.Kurkjian, D.Hamilton, J.Nester, R.Ryan,	
			W.Hengler, C.Ervin, W.Andre, F.Ghio, Ltjg J.Davies	
mid67-70	P.Haefeli	R.Childs	R.Aiken, W.Andre, J.Antink, J.Bouchard, F.Ghio,	
			A.Jarvis, E.Koller, H.Kurkjian, G.Meglemre, R.Mutch,	
			D.Hamilton, W.Hengler, B.Panico, D.Roberts, A.Wilk	
70-75	M.Hudgins	H.Bister	P.Curley, J.Eversoll, A.Keller, J.Arnold	M.Brown, J.Long
			H.Kimball, H.Ward, F.Orrantia, D.Watson	J.Dubois, N.Gomez
late78-81	R.Salmon	S.Gutshall	K.Watanabe (HL), M.Frankel, D.Karpowich, D.Lytle	
		M.Embry	L.Carroll, P.Graf, R. Painter, H.Roberts	
81-84	D.Dykes	J.S. Arnold	D.Hendrick (HL), C.Moss (HL), K.Armfield, J.Cohen	J.Skelton,
			P.Graf, M.Kishman, C.Olson, D.Perritt, D.Bradley,	D.Candanoza
			D.Depriest, T.Fisher, S.Chin, S.Volpe, B.Stamper	C.Sheehan
			R.Warmack, M.Frankel, L.Carroll--FCI	
	C.Bickley			
	K.Sumner	B.Stamper		
88-Jul 90	D.Swindle	C.Moss-Crim	M.Ridley, C.Leininger, D.See, S.Beddo, P.Houseman,	J.Skelton,
			D.Nelson, R.Sanchez, D.Otterbacher, D.Watson,	J.Washington,
			S.Rhostada, D.Bradley, D.Geiger, T.Morton, L.Chung,	D.Proctor,
			D.Houseman, S.Brady, R.Warmack, M.Giordani,	T.Onorato
			B.Nivens, F.Kroll, B.Parish, M.Relyea	D.Balk
		L.Carroll-FCI	D.Clayton, C.Rosenlund, D.Lauver, E.Jones, P.Chavez	
		C.Rivers-Fraud	J.Seay, S.Hooten, G.Bachman, N.Rich, L.Lamont, J.Lee	
			V.Cernosek, D. Watson (different), A.Panaseny, D.See	
Jul 90-Jul 93	P.Anderson	C.Moss-Crim	D.Daly, R.Mebs, D.Housman, S.Brady, D.Otterbacher	V.Otterbacher,
		L.Carroll--FCI	D.Nelson, J.Wagner, D.Watson, S.Beddo, D.Watson	T.Onorato
		P.Valentine-FCI	T.Donnelly, D.Lauver, A.Burghard, M.Relyea	D.Moore,D.Balk
Los Angeles Field Office created in July 1993				
Jul93-95	R.Miller	M.Barrett	G.Hueston, D.Rhoads, W.Brown, P.Housman,	L.Riederer,
		R.Porter-Fraud	N.Riley, P.Garza, M.Robinson, G.Bachman, J.Lee	L.Campos
			C.Panaseny, V.Cernosek, L.Amont, L.Lockwood	

10
NISRA El Toro (11ET)

Harry Reeves reported to NISRA El Toro in November 1967 shortly before Don Roberts finished his assignment as SRA and transferred to NISRA Long Beach. The office was likely established in the mid-1960s with Roberts as its first SRA. John Nester relieved Roberts according to Reeves, and was in place three to six months before Jerry Wheeler arrived as the new SRA in February 1968. Nester remained at El Toro. Harry Reeves served in various positions including ASRA off and on at NISRA EL Toro for about eight years.

As of mid 1968, the NISO San Diego roster reflects the following personnel at 11ET: Jerry Wheeler SRA, David Cogdill, Robert Maloof, John Nester, Harry Reeves, Terry Wagner, and Curtis Wickersham.

In 1971, Reeves became ASRA replacing Bob Maloof. Reeves went afloat on the USS Kitty Hawk (CV-63) from November 1973 to July 1974 before returning to El Toro as ASRA until the summer of 1975 when he departed for NISRA Subic Bay, R.P. Maynard Warwick relieved Jerry Wheeler in late 1974.

A February 1975 NISO-wide roster shows the following assigned at 11ET: SRA Warwick, Harry Reeves, Richard Allen, James Sievers, David St. Denis and Bill Hudson. Lois Suhr and Sarah Wright served as admin support. The NISRA opened a one-man office at Santa Ana in 1974 with St. Denis in that position. In mid 1976, Maynard Warwick handed the office keys to Howie Abrams who remained SRA until he was relieved by Bob Panico in 1979. Gordie Crossman was Panico's assistant.

An abbreviated NISO roster dated August 1980 shows Bob Panico at El Toro and Stan Sagara at the Santa Ana NISRU. In a similar NISO roster from 1982, the SAC is Charles Van Page while Stan Sagara is still in place as RRA Santa Ana.

In mid-1983, Randy Scott replaced Van Page as SAC. A January 1984 NISO roster lists Scott as SAC, John Cusack as ASAC, Mark Pendell as RRA Santa Ana, Special Agents R. Brechon, R. Broyles, D. Harris, and R. Murdock, GySGT L. Ervoes, SSGT W. Nereson, and administrative positions filled by E. Blaskowski, C.Clay, and J.Talbott.

Harry Stovall was assigned as SAC 11ET from June 1985 to July 1987. Towards the end of this assignment, Harry said his office was very involved in the Marine Security Guard investigation—Subject CPL Clayton Lonetree. The Co-Subject of this investigation, LCPL Bracy, had been stationed at El Toro and lived off base: thus, many hours of interviews etc. Harry also recalled that the Secretary of the Navy during this timeframe, John Lehman, was a Navy reservist who would occasionally fly into the air station thus requiring a protective service detail.

Michael Barrett became the GM-14 SAC in October 1989 and filled that position until January 1994. Barrett recalled that his office conducted several death investigations, one of which stands out-the death of the Assistant Chief of Staff (ACOS), MCAS El Toro, in early 1991. The ACOS was a USMC Colonel. Barrett said the case was worked primarily by El Toro NIS Agents, coordinated with USMC CID and the Staff Judge Advocate. The case was closed with the cause of death as suicide. A brother of the deceased did not accept the investigative findings, saying the Marine officer was murdered to prevent him telling his story about illegal drug and weapons activities of USMC members. The brother maintained the USMC, NIS and FBI all collaborated on the investigation. The case came under several JAG Manual reviews and DOD and DOJ scrutiny. As the findings did not change, the brother ultimately filed suit in the US Court of Appeals, Ninth District. After several days of testimony, the District Judge dismissed the case according to Barrett.

The March 1992 NISO San Diego Personnel Listing for the El Toro NISRA shows SAC Mike Barrett, ASAC Charles Strickland, agents Tony D'Amico, Mike Reardon, Cheryl Craycraft, Brooke Adamson, D. Sanzeri, and Melanie Sue, USMC CWO2 Vicki Lyons, SSGT Patrick O'Neal, SGT Eric Anderson, and admin support provided by Janet Talbott, Jackie Washington, and Kay Neal.

Every year, Barrett recalled, his office hosted a Law Enforcement Liaison function at the Air Station in conjunction with the annual MCAS El Toro Air Show. The guest list always included local, state, and federal law enforcement officials, and Marine PMO, CID and JAG personnel. Barrett said his office was fortunate to be able to reserve one of the small hangers close to the office and cater the event. This hanger is one of the original buildings on the base and is a historic landmark used by the Orange County Great Park to tell the history of MCAS El Toro.

Barrett recounted a story involving SA Charlie Strickland who had reported in as ASAC. Charlie had a great sense of humor. One day, Charlie brought to the office a lifesize, inflatable, Freddy Krueger look-alike doll, which was placed on one of the chairs in a lounge area of the ladies restroom. On this particular day, SAC Barrett was visited by a female FBI agent to coordinate a Presidential visit to the MCAS. The NCIS people temporarily forgot about Freddy as the FBI agent entered the ladies restroom. Hearing her scream, Charlie and Mike responded to see her holstering her weapon. She was not in a jovial mood, and Mike added that she never again made an appearance in his office.

In 1993, MCAS El Toro was designated for closing by the Base Realignment and Closure Commission and all of its activities were to be transferred to Marine Corps Air Station Miramar.

Succeeding Barrett as supervisor of 11ET but as Resident Agent in Charge (RAC) in January 1994 was seasoned agent Ken Oglesbee. Ken retained a nucleus of civilian and USMC personnel with a general caseload of seventy-five to one hundred investigations including thefts, burglaries, occasional rape and suicide. He mentioned an ongoing worker's compensation operation which targeted the fraudulent receipt of benefits. Ken also recalled the successful resolution of a case involving the shooting and wounding of a USMC CID Agent assigned to the El Toro office. The agent was shot at while running the perimeter of the base. The investigation ran for about fourteen months and was solved when an informant provided information which led to the identification of the shooter, a minor.

In October 1996, Ken Oglesbee was relieved as RAC by Ed Kunigonis. MCAS El Toro officially closed on July 2, 1999. USMC 3MAF resources were relocated to the new MCAS Miramar or Camp Pendleton and the NCIS Resident Agency was closed.

Chart 10-1 NISRA El Toro

NISRA EL TORO				
	SRA/SAC	ASRA/ASAC	OTHER AGENTS	ADMIN
66-67	D.Roberts	D. Valentine		
67-Jan 68	J.Nester	R.Maloof	D.Cogdil, H.Reeves, R.Allen, C.Wickersham	
Feb68-Nov74	J. Wheeler	R.Maloof	D.Cogdil, H.Reeves, R.Allen, C.Wickersham	L.Suhr, S.Wright
		H.Reeves	D.StDenis, W.Hudson, J.Nester, T.Wagner	
Nov74-Jul76	M.Warwick	H.Reeves	R.Allen, J.Sievers, D.StDenis, W.Hudson	L.Suhr, S.Wright
Jul76-Jul79	H.Abrams	W.Hudson		
Jul79-Jul82	R.Panico	G. Crossman	S.Sagara (SA), R.Larson, T.Clark, 4-5 others	E.Blaskowski,
Jul82-Jul83	C.Van Page		S.Sagara (SA)	
Jul83-Jun85	R. Scott	J.T. Cusack	M.Pendell (SA), R.Brechon, R.Broyles,	E. Blaskowski,
			R.Murdock, D.Harris	J.Talbott
			GySgt L.Ervoes, Ssgt W.Nereson	C.Clay
Jun85-Jul87	H.Stovall	M.Pendell	K.Watanabe (SA), K.Murphy, R.Murdock,	E.Blaskowski,
			C.Campos, six USMC CID	J.Talbott, C.Clay
Jul87-Oct89	B.Stamper	D.Depriest	K.Murphy	
Oct89-Jan94	M.Barrett	D.Depriest/	T.D'Amico, C.Craycraft, B.Adamson,	J.Talbott,
		C.Strickland	D.Sanzeri, M.Sue, M.Reardon, M.Devine	J.Washington,
			CWO2 J.Ambriz and V.Lyons, Ssgt M.Heath	K.Neal
			Ssgts P.O'Neal, E. Anderson, G.Schmidt	N.Pattee
Upon departure of SA Barrett, 11ET became part of Los Angeles Field Office				
	RAC			
Jan94-Oct96	K.Oglesbee		A.D'Amico, C.Craycraft, M.Devine,	J.Talbott
			B.Adamson, M.Sue, M.Reardon	
			M.Heath, M.Castillo, S.Bloomquist	
Oct 96-Jul99	E.Kunigonis			

11
NISRA Camp Pendleton (11PE)

Before NIS, the ONI San Diego office conducted all investigative activity at Camp Pendleton. According to Roy Mosteller, one agent was assigned to handle all North County including Camp Pendleton investigative work for a one year assignment and that meant driving there every day from San Diego. When Roy had this assignment, he remembers going to the Supervising Agent Charles Morehead and saying, "There is lots and lots of criminal work at Camp Pendleton being done by the Marines. Why are we not doing it?" Morehead solemnly replied, "Roy, don't rock the boat." ONI continued to concentrate on Personnel Security Investigations (PSI).

In October 1964, Senior Resident Agent (SRA) Jim Byrd, Special Agents Harry Stovall, Bob Grossman, Don Deuville and a female secretary established the Camp Pendleton ONI office and became "Plank Owners." Their office was a Butler Hut at the top of Rattlesnake Canyon, collocated with the USMC CID office. In early 1965, Bill Phillip reported onboard and Stovall departed in May 1965. The workload remained mainly PSIs with an increasing number of criminal investigations. In the 1966-67 period, the NISRA had outgrown its Butler Hut and moved into a WWII barracks, building 1224.

The 1968 NISO-wide personnel roster lists the following at Camp Pendleton: SRA Bill Gray, Charles Bickley, George Carpenter, Don Dombrowski, John Keefe, Doug Laird, Murray Mahan, Richard Mesa, William Philip, Byron Taylor, Vern White, and J.M. Woolery.

Pete Reilly reported in as ASRA to Bill Gray in March 1969 and continued in that capacity with Roy Mosteller who became the third SRA in August 1970. Pete Reilly, who was a GS-12 at the time, has said that NISRA Camp Pendleton was one of the first Category 1 NISRAs and that Bill Gray was the first GS-13 SRA assigned. Mosteller recalls that in the late 1970 to early 1971 period, the 1st Marine Division returned from Vietnam, and brought the war home with them. Assaults and homicides became nearly every-day occurrences. Roy recalled an incident from his 1971/72 Camp Pendleton days when someone broke into the office evidence room and stole some marijuana. Entry was gained through an evidence room window which had been painted to look like the wall and was not realized by the NIS people.

Old NIS Office Building 1224

Perhaps his most memorable day, Roy recalls, was the visit of President Richard Nixon to Camp Pendleton to review the recently returned 1st Marine Division. When a President visits a Navy or Marine Corps installation, it is normal for the US Secret Service to request NIS assistance. On this occasion, all of the 11PE agents assisted the Secret Service. As the President departed the ceremonies, hundreds of spectators rushed to see him, and Roy became pinned against President Nixon's vehicle. Roy found himself unable to move and helpless with his arms pinned against his side by the throngs of people. Roy Mosteller served there until late 1972 when he was relieved by Roger Teel.

Doug Stuart was one of about thirteen agents that populated the 11PE office during the early 1970s, working for SRAs Gray, Mosteller and Teel. Stuart remembered the following MCB Camp Pendleton Enlisted Club arson incident as he was the principal investigating agent. One night circa 1973, the Twenty-four area Enlisted Club burned to a total loss. The club was housed in a wood frame, single story structure of about 15,000 square feet. Initial response by NCIS revealed a very hot, fast moving fire that gave strong indication of use of an accelerant. Within a few hours, the cause of arson was firmly established. Not only were there sufficient indicators of a liquid accelerant, a partially filled can of gasoline was found upside down on the floor of the bar room.

The floor was totally cleared and revealed graphic evidence that the gasoline had been poured through the adjoining ball and bar room and set alight. It appeared the arsonist must have thrown an ignition source though a window from the outside or he would have probably suffered severe burns. One window near the point of origin was found to have been open during the fire (but was reported closed and locked the previous day).

Gasoline evidence along with appropriate samples was sent to the Naval Laboratory at Port Hueneme for analysis by gas chromatograph. It was subsequently established the fuel was pumped from the Marine Corps Exchange service station in the Thirteen area.

Interviews of virtually every person in the Twenty-four area as well as persons developed as visitors on the night of the fire were done without any significant information. An interview of a marine who occupied a Twenty-four area barracks produced positive results. This marine was awaked during the night of the fire by a roommate who was spraying his clothes with deodorant. When asked why he was doing this, the roommate replied that he was getting rid of the gasoline odor on his clothes.

The suspect was interrogated and eventually confessed he had burned down the club to take revenge on a senior NCO who had somehow offended him. This confession was partially corroborated by his description of syphoning fuel from a particular car. The owner of the car confirmed the gasoline came from the Thirteen area gas station. The suspect was tried and convicted at General Courts Martial.

Brian McKee served as SRA from 1974 to 1975 with Chuck Bickley as his Assistant. One significant experience identified by Brian was the relocation of Vietnam refugees to Camp Pendleton which prompted a visit by Mrs. Gerald Ford to the refugee camp. Brian advised that crimes of violence continued to dominate the case workload. In reaction to the many after-hours duty calls, Brian said his office began a second shift, five in the afternoon to one in the morning, to the great consternation of headquarters.

As of September 1974, there were thirteen Special Agents and three support personnel supervised by Brian McKee at NISRA Camp Pendleton.

Brian McKee departed in mid-1975 to relieve Warren Lynch as SRA in New York. Chuck Bickley became the acting 11PE SRA for a month or so until Wes Howe arrived as the new manager of the office. In August or September 1975, Don Laughton came in to replace Bickley as the ASRA. One of the street agents who provided continuity during this timeframe was John Hopeck who had come onboard as an agent in February 1975 and remained at 11PE until July 1979. Sometime in 1977, according to Hopeck, Bob Kain relieved Wes Howe as SRA.

Another continuity street agent during this timeframe was Ken Oglesbee who began his NIS career as a GS-7 at 11PE in October 1974 and remained there until July 1976 working general criminal cases. Ken recalls his typical workload as ten to twenty cases across the spectrum of crimes against persons and property. Ken remembers the first time that he was Duty Agent by himself, he opened seven investigations that he kept and one or two that got passed to other agents in his twenty-four hour assignment. Ken advised that 11PE was a great office for first assignment agents, citing fantastic senior agent mentors Jim Kiker, Pete Anderson, Roy Elmquist, Bill Nugent, and Jack Givens; great supervisors in McKee and Bickley; and very competent co-workers.

Following Bob Kain as Special Agent in Charge (SAC) was Bud Aldridge in the January 1982 to January 1984 timeframe. The SAC title had replaced SRA as the term used for the supervisor of the Resident Agency. Bud recalled that he was in this assignment for two years, "almost to the day." He then was transferred to the SAC position at Marine Corps Base Camp Lejeune, N.C. Bud says he believes he is the only person to have filled the SAC position at both major Marine Corps bases, and definitely is the only NIS/NCIS person to have filled those positions back to back.

Doug Stuart returned to Camp Pendleton in 1984 for his second tour—this time as the SAC. Doug's predecessor, Bud Aldridge, began Operation RipStop which continued during Doug's regime. RipStop, which was worked with the FBI, targeted "surplus" dealers purchasing equipment stolen from Camp Pendleton. The operation utilized undercover agents and a storefront business. According to Stuart, RipStop was compromised when an FBI affidavit for a search warrant which was supposedly sealed was found by a reporter. Doug noted that every military suspect who was prosecuted was convicted before the first civilian trial was begun.

In January 1984, NISO San Diego identified sixteen Special Agents, four active duty marines, and six admin support employed at Camp Pendleton. By March 1992, these numbers grew to seventeen agents, five marines, and seven admin support.

Vince Giame served as SAC probably longer than any other person—from July 1989 to March 1996. He recalls this duty as a great assignment with plenty of good cases to work and a bunch of dedicated, hard working agents to do it. Vince also noted they worked in an old World War II building that should have been condemned. The office building that Vince is talking about is the same that Roy Mosteller told us about. Since 1967, ONI/NIS/NCIS occupied historic Camp Pendleton building 1224 which was pictured earlier.

NISRA Camp Pendleton 1992

Ed Jex had a unique assignment from August 1995 to August 2000 as the NCIS representative to the North San Diego County Gang Task Force, which was co-located with the Oceanside Police Department. The Task Force conducted four of the largest gang narcotic operations in county history to include the single largest black tar heroin case in US history at that time.

For a period of time in the mid to late 1990s, the Camp Pendleton office became operational under the San Diego or Southwest Field Office. As such, the office supervisor was titled Resident Agent in Charge or RAC rather than SAC.

From January 1996 to September 1997, Steve Kahl was assigned as the RAC. Steve reported that his office averaged sixty rape cases per year and a death investigation every ten days. Steve recalled a pleasant incident when he went to brief the 1st Marine Division Assistant Division Commander. As he was waiting to meet the officer, Steve realized that he knew BGEN John Todd and had served with the latter in Okinawa in 1971. In moves that Steve still cannot understand, his agent strength started at twenty-four and was allowed to taper to seventeen during his tenure despite his strenuous objections to the SW Field Office and NCIS Headquarters. According to Steve, Camp Pendleton was the busiest office in NCIS during this time. On the day that Cliff Link relieved Steve as RAC, three additional Special Agents were assigned to Camp Pendleton according to Steve.

During the January 1994 to May 1998 timeframe while Vince Giame was SAC and Steve Kahl and Cliff Link served as RAC, Bruce Smart served in various capacities as ASAC, SSA, and Assistant RAC.

Dan Simas, who served as 11PE RAC in the 1999-2001 period, provided the following information on two homicide investigations. After more than a decade following the discovery of a woman's body found floating in Lake O'Neil onboard Camp Pendleton, information surfaced identifying a possible suspect. Using that information, a cold case homicide investigation conducted by Special Agent Julie Haney was begun. With a New Orleans, LA, Police Department Lieutenant as an undercover agent (UCA), arrangements were made to have the UCA placed on a Mississippi riverboat on which the suspect was employed. In a short period of time, the UCA gained the suspect's trust, and he confessed to the UCA how he had killed the woman and dumped her body into Lake O'Neil. Because the killing of the woman, a local prostitute, occurred off base, the case was prosecuted by the San Diego District Attorney's Office. The suspect was found guilty and sentenced to prison. Special Agent Haney was given an award for her outstanding skills in putting this case together.

Another case involved the murder of a wife by her active duty US Navy husband, a corpsman assigned to the base hospital. He threw his wife's body into a slough on base which resulted in her remains being strewn about base housing by wild animals. The corpsman and his girlfriend, also a corpsman, were found guilty of murder.

Dan Simas commented that he felt Camp Pendleton is where Special Agents become premier investigators. The myriad of cases investigated by the SAs far exceeds other offices. Those who began their careers at Camp Pendleton normally excelled and developed into outstanding leaders.

In 2001, SA Mark Ridley was assigned as the RAC. Two years later, NCISRA Camp Pendleton became the Marine Corps West Field Office (MCWFO) and Mark Ridley was selected as the SAC. At that time, there were forty-five SAs and eight administrative support personnel at the MCWFO. The MCWFO was responsible for NCIS activities at MCB Camp Pendleton, Marine Corps Air Station (MCAS) Miramar, Marine Corps Recruit Depot San Diego, and MCAS Yuma, Arizona. SA Ridley recently retired as the Deputy Director of NCIS.

NCIS Headquarters implemented a new program in December 2001 wherein experienced retired Special Agents were rehired as annuitants to perform various administrative duties including new agent background screening. The first retired SAs to be sent to Camp Pendleton were Larry Ferrell and Ray Larabee. Ferrell later became the FOSO at MCWFO, a position in which he served until retiring again in August 2008.

In late 2002, Mark Ridley directed annuitant Larry Ferrell to initiate efforts to find a more suitable building to house the NCIS Office. Larry said that about ten million dollars in funds from NCIS and Marine Corp Base were identified. Building plans were developed and construction began about September 2008. Construction was monitored by Field Operation Support Officer (FOSO) Kathy Hampton, SAC's Jewel Seawood, Chris Cote and Gregg Munroe, and NCIS Director Mark Clookie. The building was completed April 2010 as the first Field Office built from the ground up to become operational in NCIS history.

MCWFO building completed 2010

When Mark Ridley was transferred to NCIS Headquarters in early 2004, Jewel Seawood was promoted to GS-15 to become SAC of the MCWFO. Jewel had come full circle in her NIS/ NCIS career, having begun such as a GS-7 Special Agent working general criminal cases at Camp Pendleton twenty years earlier. In her two and one-half year assignment as MCWFO SAC, Jewel said the most significant case was not a case controlled by the Field Office but a case controlled by another component of NCIS. It was the investigation conducted into the massacre of twenty-four civilians in Haditha, Iraq, in November 2005, by USMC members. NCIS Investigation was not requested until March 2006. MCWFO played a significant role in the subsequent investigation as all the suspects and witnesses were marines assigned to Camp Pendleton. A task force of about forty agents, analysts and support personnel from MCWFO and the Southwest Field Office was formed and worked the investigative leads. Jewel Seawood and her ASAC supervised the task force. Much has been written in the open press about this incident, the various investigations into and about it, and resultant actions.

From 2006 to 2008, SA Christopher W. Cote served as the SAC of MCWFO. He directed all criminal, counter terrorism and criminal investigative operations in support of Marine Corps Installations West and the First Marine Expeditionary Force. He is currently Executive Assistant Director for Intelligence and Information Sharing, NCIS Headquarters.

In 2010, manning levels at MCWFO consisted of about eighty Special Agents and fourteen administrative support personnel. Gregg Munroe was the SAC. Resident Agencies were located at MCAS Miramar supervised by J. Dela Cruz, MCB Twentynine Palms headed by D.Carlin, MCAS Yuma with RAC J.Barron, Polygraph Unit led by R.Baloun, and Support Staff supervised by FOSO K. Hampton.

Following Munroe was Susan Simon who was assigned as SAC of MCWFO from 2010 to March 2012 and then SAC of the Southwest Field Office from March 2012 to May 2014. Susan Simon was relieved in the MCWFO SAC position by Chuck Warmuth. Warmuth, who retired from NCIS in December 2016, told the writer that his office typically carried a caseload of 350-400 pending cases at any time divided amongst fifty-five to sixty-five agents, aided by eight to ten professional support personnel. The Field Office currently maintains Resident Agencies at MCAS Miramar, MCAS Yuma, MCB Twentynine Palms and a Resident Unit at NAS Fallon, NV. At Camp Pendleton, according to Chuck Warmuth, much of their current workload is focused on the forty thousand or so Marine Corps personnel and dependents who reside on base.

Chart 11-1 NISRA Camp Pendleton

NISRA CAMP PENDLETON (11PE)				
	SRA/SAC	ASRA/ASAC	OTHER AGENTS	ADMIN
Oct64-66	J.Byrd	none	H.Stovall, R.Grossman, D.Deuville, W.Phillip	
66-Jun 70	W. Gray	P.Reilly	C.Bickley, G.Carpenter, D.Dombrowski, J.Keefe, D.Laird	
			M.Mahan, R.Mesa, W.Philip, B.Taylor, V.White, T.Miller	
Jun70-Oct72	R.Mosteller	P.Reilly	D.Stuart, J.Woolery, J.Schroeder, T.Brannon, T.Miller,	
			C.Bickley, W.Clayton, C.Cole, P.Cook, R.Woelffer, R.Mesa	
Oct72-Jun74	R. Teel	C.Bickley	D.Stuart, W.Nugent, R.Janson, T.Brannon, J.Schroeder,	
			R.Mesa, J.Woolery, A.Hooser, F.Grim, J.Givens	
Jun74-Jun75	J.B. McKee	C. Bickley	P.Anderson, R.Elmquest, J.Givens, R.Hardy,	K.Gerfen,
			A.Hooser, R.Janson, W.Nugent, R.Peters, W.Homberg,	J. La Freniere
			F.Grim, J.Hopeck, K.Oglesbee, J.Kiker, P.Cook, D.Heintz,	S.Guill
Jun75-Jun77	W.Howe	C.Bickley	P.Anderson, P.Cook, R.Elmquest, J.Givens, J.Chambers,	
		D.Laughton	R.Hardy, J.Hopeck, F.Grim	
Aug77-Jan82	R.Kain	T.Tate		
Jan82-Jan84	G. Aldridge	T.Tate/R.Rainville	R.Lorch(SK),S.Reed,H.Garcia,D.Heintz,M.Corrigan,R.Lucas	J.Heard,
			J.Chambers,T.D'Amico,S.Freeman,F.Edmonds,R.McSherry,	M.Slate
			K.Frestel,C.Calhoun,H.Jiminez,D.Galante,F.Kaufman	C.Freeman
			G.Helson,J.O'Neil,WO M.Tuck,WO R.Williams,Ssgt R.Otto	
Jan84-Nov86	D.Stuart	R.Rainville	S.Reed (SK), C.Calhoun, R.Crizer, A.D'Amico, K.Murphy,	P.Bullger,
		T.Perrin	F.Kauffman, T.Hustler, J.McNaught, M.Clark, J.Seawood,	D.Flora, L.Rebar,
			D.Shuck,D.Einsel,J.Marsh,R.McSherry,J.Moller,D.Heintz	S.Maile, M.Slate
			R.Stripay, B.Dolinka, J.Felton, M.Corrigan, M.Kachlin	C.Galloway
			J.O'Neil,1st Lt Tuck,Ssgt H.Garcia,Ssgt R.Loe,Ssgt R.Otto	J.Heard,
Nov86-Nov87	D.Dykes			
Nov87-Jul89	J.Marquette	R.Lorch/J.Mann		S.Maile
Jul89-Mar96	V.Giami	R.Lorch-Crim	M.Shanley, W.Jacobson, D.Yery, R.Richardson, R.Bolden,	S.Maile, L.Rebar
		J.Mann-FCI	C.Calhoun, C.Alvarez, M.Liptak, D.Parnell, T.LaCosta,E.Jex	L.Heard, N.Patee,
			D.Russell,M.Fahey,J.Haney,A.Spafford,S.Larraway,M.Rich	A.Egelund,
			D.Heintz, K.Veria, R.Bolden, T.LaCosta, P.Hicks, G.Hood	S.Kennedy,
			D.Raser,J.Wagner,J.Barron, M.Geyer, P.Byrne,P.Hurt	T.Jordan-Evdnce
			WO B.Russell,WO Johnson,Gysgt B.Lewis,SSgt L.Peterson	
11PE became subordinate to the San Diego Field Office when SAC Giami departed.				
Jan96-Sep97	RAC S.Kahl	R.Lorch		
Sep97-Jul99	RAC C.Link			
July99-May01	RAC D.Simas		J.Wagner,M.Thompson,J.Wagner,J.Diaz,E.Jex,M.Cote	A.Egelund
			D.Heintz,M.Acevedo,M.Nach,M.Bradford,B.Yankowski	
			M.Fahey,D.Harris,J.Kuhrt,T.Flores,E.Fenner, M.Liptak	
Marine Corps West Field Office established				
01--Apr04	M.Ridley			K.Hampton,
Apr04-Oct06	J.Seawood	D.Cooper-Crim	M.Liptack, K.Proffitt, M.Reese,	L.Ferrell,
		J.McDougal-FCI	K.Marks, G.Bachman--all SSAs	A.Ferguson
Oct06-Mar09	C.Cote			K.Hampton,
Mar09-Jun10	G. Munroe		J.Delacruz (MM), D.Carlin (TN), J.Barron (YU)	K.Hampton,
Sep10-Mar12	S.Simon			K.Hampton,
Mar12-Dec16	C.Warmuth	B.Platt		K.Hampton,

12
NISRA San Diego (11SD)/NISRA Point Loma (11PL)

Prior to February 1966, the DIO staff conducted background and criminal investigations involving Navy and Marine Corps members. Pat Daly is known to have been the SRA of the DIO San Diego staff as of 1963 when Dick Childs and Harry Stovall were hired as Special Agents. George Reis was already in place as a polygraph examiner. Dick Childs was assigned to the "Informal Criminal Squad" as he puts it in San Diego until his transfer to NISRA Long Beach in January 1967. Childs remembers that Pat Daly was the SRA when NISRA San Diego was created in February 1966 and was still in that position as of January 1967. Sometime later, Ken Seal relieved Pat Daly as SRA.

A 1968 NISO San Diego roster shows Ken Seal as SRA in charge of about twenty civilian agents and two USN Officer agents. That same roster shows Ken Seal transferring to Charleston, SC, in August 1968. According to George Reis, Seal was relieved as SRA by Pete Hansen who remained in that position until he was succeeded by Roy Mosteller. George Reis added that he served as ASRA to both Ken Seal and Pete Hansen.

In July1972, Roy Mosteller became SRA of NISRA San Diego which covered all of the city outside of the USN/USMC bases. He remained in that position for three years with Dick Wardman as his ASRA. At that time, the NISRA was collocated with NISO San Diego at 3250 Fordham St., San Diego. NISRA San Diego leaders also supervised NIS Residence Units (NISRU) at Barstow (11BW), China Lake (11CK), Ballast Point (11BL), San Diego Naval Hospital (11HB), and Twenty-Nine Palms (11TN). These were all normally one-man offices. Agent reports came to Mosteller for review before dissemination and he periodically inspected each NISRU. Very few agents were assigned to NISRA San Diego at this time because most of the Navy facilities in San Diego were onboard bases covered by other NIS offices. Therefore, most of NISRA San Diego's investigative work was covering leads in the city generated from NIS offices outside of San Diego.

In February 1975 as documented in a NISO personnel roster, Mosteller, Wardman, Joe McClure, Gerry Strauss (11BL), Mike Evans, Al Jesse (11BL), James Antink (11BW), Paul Clark (11CK), Bryan Cook, Steve Spears, Bob L'Heureux, and Larry Skinner were assigned agents and Penny Shosted and Karen Springer were admin personnel.

After Roy Mosteller retired in July 1975, Don Hartman came is as SAC, and Archie Hooser came down from NISRA Camp Pendleton to become his ASAC. By early 1979, NISRA San Diego moved five miles south and became NISRA Point Loma (11PL). The office was located in the old barracks area of the Naval Ocean Systems Center (NOSC) at the top of the peninsula with the Pacific Ocean on one side and San Diego Bay on the other and the Point Loma lighthouse a mile or so down the road. The NOSC was one of the Navy's scientific laboratories—lots of engineers and scientists doing lots of sensitive and sometimes highly classified work and correspondingly—lots of money. NISRA Point Loma was headed by one of the legends of NIS, a gentleman named R.K.G. Rende, known as Bob. Bob was a big man who smoked cigars and drove a big Lincoln automobile. Most every day, Bob would gather up several agents who would pile in the big Lincoln for the short ride to a favorite sandwich shop on the Pacific side of Point Loma.

The NIS work at NOSC was pretty much thefts of government property, but with lots of money came incidents of fraud and the NISRA became more and more involved in these cases.

In 1980, several NIS offices nationwide to include Point Loma housed agents who were assigned to Navy Material Command activities, Supply Centers, and Navy Laboratories. At 11PL, the Fraud Squad was established comprised of Special Agents Rod Staudinger, Grant McIntosh, Kim Myers, and Allan Sipe, each of whom was assigned one or more of the Navy's major procurement or material commands and dedicated to development of procurement fraud cases. Over the next couple of years, 11PL conducted several major fraud investigations--two of which involved a senior official of NOSC and the owner of a ship repair company who overbilled the Navy for his work. As the program developed, fraud-dedicated NISRAs were established at Point Loma and Los Angeles in 1987 as described later.

In mid-1981, Bob Rende got orders overseas and was replaced by Howie Abrams as SAC. Howie brought many years of fraud investigation expertise to the office. Another new addition was Sam Knowles who reported in as ASAC.

One day, Sam came to work, got his coffee, and went to his office only to find that his desk had been removed and all the items from the top of his desk had been neatly arranged on the floor. Without saying a word, Sam sat on the floor and began conducting business as if nothing was different. The agents responsible for this rearrangement had left behind two chairs in which they sat while conducting the day's business with Sam.

Another major change at 11PL occurred in 1983 with the startup of the Foreign Counterintelligence (FCI) program. That year, the Central Intelligence Agency provided NIS Headquarters with financing which enabled NIS to fund FCI activities. Approximately seventy agents became dedicated throughout NIS. NISO San Diego implemented this program by starting FCI Squads at NISRAs Long Beach and Point Loma. At 11PL, the squad consisted of Allan Sipe as Squad Leader, Tom Kozlowski, Kevin Keating, and Robin Parks. Sometime later, Robin and Allan became engaged in a sensitive, highly classified investigation involving a NOSC official. At one point, they drafted a Naval message which was classified secret and written with code words and pseudonyms to protect the individuals/situations/sources. They took the message to the new ASAC, Byron Taylor, for release and Byron refused to do so if he could not be briefed in on the investigation. After being told that the message was urgent and had to be released, Byron signed the release but only under the condition that the matter be discussed with the SAC Howie Abrams. The next day, the matter was presented to Howie who decided that Byron would not be briefed in on the investigation.

A January 1984 NISO roster shows the following at NISRA Point Loma: SAC Abrams, ASAC Dan Simas, RRA Allan Sipe, Jim Chamber, Katie Frestel, Tom Koslowski, Kim Myers, Mike Nixon, Tim Butts and Steve Kahl at Ballast Point, ENS R.Musico, USN, and admin persons Nancy Kohler and Jan Dehart. In the Spring of 1984 as office space at 11PL was limited, the FCI Squad relocated to MCRD San Diego where there was a detached office large enough to accommodate four agents and one secretary.

NISRA Point Loma operated a one or two person satellite office at Ballast Point, home of two squadrons of attack submarines, two submarine tenders, and supporting shore establishment. Typically, the NIS agents were kept busy with property crimes and narcotic/dangerous drug investigations. Steve Kahl filled this position in the 1983-84 timeframe. He was assisted by Joe McDonough, a young agent and former Missouri police officer with no military experience. Kahl took McDonough with him to brief the Commanding Officer of a sub tender about a case. Kahl told his protégé to watch and listen. The suspect was a sailor assigned to the engine room of the ship and Kahl repeatedly referred to him as Fireman Smith, denoting the man's rate and rating as a non-petty officer. At one point looking confused, McDonough commented, "I didn't know there was a fire department on a ship like this."

Kahl recalled another case in which a .45 caliber pistol was reported missing from an attack submarine. While divers were searching the water around the submarine, Kahl proceeded with his investigation, identified a suspect, obtained a confession, located and retrieved the missing weapon onboard the sub.

In the mid 1980s, the Navy was constructing a huge new hospital in Balboa Park. Steve Kahl decided to focus on fraud cases at the hospital. He developed an excellent relationship with the Resident Officer in Charge of Construction, Captain McConnell, who was a brusque older Navy Engineering Officer who wanted to see the Navy get full value for dollars. He would tell contractors that Kahl was active on the site for an effective deterrent effect. To support this effect, Kahl was frequently at the site talking with workers both government and contractors. And he did find issues to work.

The best case came from a government contract administrator who oversaw concrete work. In the back of the new hospital was a canyon, at the bottom of which was a creek bed. A major roadway to access the hospital was at the bottom of the canyon on the opposite side of the creek bed, requiring a bridge over the streambed. The upper side of this concrete structure required an apron from deep under the streambed so that when the water was high, it would not scour out under the bridge. The ambulance entrance was across this bridge, so it was critical that this access be available. The contractor for the bridge was having trouble attaining adequate soil compaction for the type of soil under the apron of the bridge, holding up the required progress. The government inspector told Kahl that he had been approached by the company foreman who offered a bribe to falsify the soil compaction test.

With the NIS technical services agent, Kahl wired the inspector for a meeting with the foreman and company president. They renewed their offer to the inspector. As Kahl filmed the meeting, the foreman drew a number, the amount of the offered bribe, in the sand with his boot. It was visible on the video. After debriefing the inspector, Kahl obtained a federal grand jury indictment from the Assistant US Attorney and assembled a team of about twelve agents to make the arrests. Kahl and another agent found the foreman down the slope from the road where the apron was being prepared and arrested him, handcuffing him there. He was somewhat belligerent, but they led him up the slope to a NIS car and transport to the federal correctional facility in San Diego where he was booked. Meanwhile, the arrest team that went to the company headquarters brought in the president. After reviewing the evidence, both the president and foreman plead guilty and received prison sentences. The company was debarred from federal contracts. Captain McConnell was very pleased and used this example to other contractors. Kahl gives him credit as being one of the few senior military commanders who really were happy to have professional fraud investigators.

In 1985, Howie Abrams was relieved and retired from NIS. In the next two years or so,

Point Loma fraud efforts were led by Doug Tomaso followed by Ted Hicks. Neither had much fraud investigative experience. Finally in September 1987, Regional Director Win Kuehl effected a flip-flop transfer of experienced fraud investigator Ernie Simon coming to Point Loma from Miramar and Ted Hicks returning to the Naval Air Station, Miramar.

By this time, fraud expertise had been established at NISRA Point Loma such that criminal investigation responsibilities and personnel were moved over to NISRA Training Commands and major procurement fraud investigations became the norm for the new Fraud Unit San Diego or 11FD. Ernie Simon and Cliff Link, both experienced fraud investigators, lead the effort.

In April 1990, Steve Kahl was promoted to GM-14 and became the second and last SAC of the Fraud Unit San Diego. A year later, Glenn Logan replaced Cliff Link as ASAC. Together, Kahl and Logan supervised a group of about fourteen other agents as they continued to probe into suspected fraud at major procurement activities in the San Diego area. As the San Diego Field Office became operational in the 1993-94 timeframe, the Fraud Unit was disestablished. Steve Kahl became ASAC for Fraud under SAC Frank Melia, and the Fraud Unit personnel were moved from Point Loma to the new Field Office facility onboard Naval Station, San Diego.

Chart 12-1 NISRA San Diego/Point Loma

NISRA San Diego (11SD)/Point Loma (11PL)/Fraud Unit (11FD)				
	SRA/SAC	ASRA/ASAC	OTHER AGENTS	ADMIN
??-Aug 68	K. Seal	G.Reis	H.Abrams, J.Beauparlant, J.Britt, G.Brooks,	
			E.Hella, R.Johnstone, A.Jesse, C.Pierpoint,	
			R.Steel, W.Sumner, R.Taylor, R.Usher,	
			F.Grim, T.Marxs & J.Hennenhoefer (USN)	
			W.Focht, R.Freeman, R.Roberts, F.Stillwell	
			A.vonMaucher, R.Wall, T.Love, J.Weaver	
Aug68-Jul72	P.Hansen	G.Reis		
Jul72-Jul75	R. Mosteller	F.Givens	G.Allen, J.Beauparlant, J. Britt, R.Freeman,	C.Morris,
			M.Hawkins, F.Lynch, T.Henderson,	B.Baker
			M.Chiuminatto, K.Weaver, R.Steel, P.Clark (CK)	C.Leonnard
			V.McDonld (BW), J.McClure (HB), H.Lingan (TN)	
	R.Mosteller	R.Wardman	B.Cook (HB), M.Evans (BL), L.Skinner (TN)	B.Baker,
			LT D.Hershberger, R.L'Heureux (TN), P.Clark (CK)	K.Springer
			LT M.Lingo, A.Jesse (BL), T.Henderson (BL)	E.Grant
			S.Spears (HB), J.Antink (BW), J.McClure (HB)	D.Marchok,
Jul75-Dec78	D.Hartman	A.Hooser	S.Spears (HB), V.McPherson (BL), B.Cook	K. Springer
			D.Driscol, S.Hastings, M.Evans	P.Shosted
Dec78-Jun81	R.Rende	A.Hooser	D.Driscol (BL), D. Wappes, D.Heintz, T.Butts,	K.Jesse,
			T.Kozlowski, A.Sipe (BL), R.Staudinger, S.Ellis	N.Kohler
		S.Knowles	J.Demaggio, K.Keating, R.Cloonan, F.Walsh,	K.Springer
Jun81-Jul85	H.Abrams	B.Taylor	A.Sipe, T.Kozlowski, R.Parks, K.Keating--all FCI	N.Kohler,
		D.Simas	J.Chambers, K.Frestel, K.Myers, M.Nixon, M.Orr,	J.Dehart
			T.Butts (BL), S.Kahl, J.McDonough, L.Vellucci,	
			T.Malloch, R.Musico, D.Cooper, R.Klienman	
Jul85-Oct86	D.Tomaso	S.Ferguson		
Oct86-Sep87	T.Hicks	C.Link	M.Orr, D.Cooper, S.Kellum	N.Kohler
Fraud Unit San Diego				
Sep87-Apr90	E.Simon	C.Link		
Apr90-Jan93	S.Kahl	C.Link	J.Deguzman, R.Vaisa, J.Moss, G.Carruth, J.Kuhrt,	N.Kohler,
		G.Logan	J.Tackett, J.Crosby, S.Kolodji, T.Piper, K Hayes	E.Pansaniban
			J.Kuhrt, M.Acevedo, M.Sweeney, A.Peterson	J.Cantley
Became part of San Diego Field Office				

13
NISRA Miramar (11MM)

Dan Foley was assigned as the first SRA of NISRA Miramar from January 1972 to November 1975. He came from duty as SRA Pasadena. Naval Air Station (NAS) Miramar was previously serviced by agents from NISRA San Diego. At the time of the opening of NISRA Miramar, the office was housed in the back of the Acey Deucy Enlisted Club. Original office agents (Plank Owners) were Dan Foley, Kirby Sumner, Byron Taylor, Fred Stilwell, and Gary Hall. They later moved to Building 254, an office in the Navy Exchange Building on Mitscher Way just inside the North gate of the Air Station.

1972 NISRA Miramar

In about 1973, the first of many NISO San Diego annual golf tournaments was held at NAS Miramar. The first foursome consisted of Capt. Nello Pirozzi, USN, former Blue Angel and Commanding Officer of the Navy Drug Rehab Center, Miramar, SA Byron Taylor of NISRA Miramar, SA Matt Hudgins of NISRA Long Beach, and SA Sherm Bliss, Supervising Agent of NISO San Diego.

Golfers 1973—Capt. Pirozzi,B.Tayor, M.Hudgins, S.Bliss

A February 1975 NISO San Diego roster shows the following agents at NISRA Miramar: Dan Foley, Al Deahl, Paul Cook, Gerald Hall, Steve Kahl, Jim Pender, Lt Mike Lingo, USN, and administrative personnel LeNor

Covert and Penny Tomlinson.

In November 1975, Dick Wardman relieved Foley who was transferred to Subic Bay, RP as SRA of Operation Scoutmaster/Stableboy.

Richard Sullivan, who was hired as a Special Agent in January 1976, provided the following about Sandra DeLuca who is thought to be one of the first women to be designated an NIS Special Agent. Sandy, as she was called, was an active duty Naval Officer married to a Navy Dentist. Circa 1973-1975, Sandy had been the Disciplinary Officer at Naval Station Rota, Spain, where she knew and worked with Jim Pender. Sandy had gone to NIS Basic School sometime in 1974 or 1975 and she became the second of two Naval Officer agents (with Mike Lingo) assigned to 11MM. Sandy was a very competent and skilled Special Agent and gladly pitched in with Sullivan's training. Sometime in 1977 or 1978, Sandy's husband completed his active duty, Sandy resigned her commission, and they moved back east.

In late 1976, Ken Oglesbee transferred from NISRA Camp Pendleton to NISRA Miramar.

Despite the sometimes intense work pressure in a NIS office, there is time for occasional humor. According to Dick Sullivan, ASRA Al Deahl would field all incoming calls from the base and agents knew when he had a real "hummer" of a case. Dick said he could hear Al tell the command, "I'll get one of my best agents on it." "It" was usually a hot stolen toolbox case or the theft of an Advance Model HT-210 Vacuum Cleaner (government loss value $101.00) from one of the squadron barracks. In self-protection, Ken Oglesbee and Dick devised a system of "Hummer Alerts" complete with sound effects from the "Victory at Sea" soundtrack, a Federal Fireball emergency revolving red light and old air-raid warden hats. They would sound the Hummer alert, stuff their trousers into their socks and kill the lights. From time to time, Al would decide just to take the "hummer" case for himself.

Harry Stovall reported to 11MM and SRA Dick Wardman in June 1977. Harry recalls a full criminal caseload with a mingling of FCI. For several years beginning in the late 1970s, the NISRA sponsored a law enforcement liaison event on the Friday of the Miramar Air show. The NISRA hosted invitees at the flight line to watch the performance, then to the Officer's Club for beverages. Stovall said the base had two prominent Navy officers onboard during this timeframe. The NAS Miramar Executive Officer was Capt. Cole Black, an aviator who was held as a POW by the North Vietnamese for several years, and the Commanding Officer of Top Gun, Capt. Duke Cunningham, who was later to become a US congressman

For many years, NAS Miramar was the West Coast home of the US Navy fighter airplane squadrons and Airborne Early Warning, E-2C Hawkeye, squadrons. It was also the home of the Fighter Weapons Training School--Top Gun--and served as main base as the Navy transitioned from the F-4 Phantom to the F-14 Tomcat.

Warren Lynch came onboard ONI in 1961 after serving in the USMC during World War II and Korean conflict and employment with the Los Angeles Police Department. Warren had one local NIS assignment as SAC of NISRA Miramar from 1979 when he relieved Dick Wardman to 1981 when he retired from NIS.

Serving as Warren's ASAC for the later part of his assignment was Ted Hicks who became part of two switches of leadership in the region and at NISRA Miramar. In January 1981, Ted and Harry Stovall flip-flopped assignments: Harry went to the SARDO position at NISO San Diego and Ted left that duty to become Miramar ASAC. Hicks carried the transition of 11MM from Warren Lynch to his relief, Marshall Whidden who filled the SAC role for about two years.

Larry Ferrell served as SAC from July 1983 to November 1986. The January 1984 NISRO San Diego roster shows the following 11MM personnel: Larry Ferrell, Gary Helson, Mark Fox, Irene Howard, Art Spafford, Bernie Yankowski, and admin personnel J.McCarthy and K.McClone.

In September 1987, Ted Hicks became part of his second flip-flop. This time, he left his position as SAC of NISRA Point Loma to become the Miramar SAC and Ernie Simon, who had filled the Miramar position for a little over one year, moved over to Point Loma.

NISRA Miramar 1984 L to R B.Yankowski, G.Helson, M.Fox, L.Ferrell, I.Howard

Bruce Smart was the last SAC, serving from June 1990 to August 1992 when he moved to the 11HQ to become the Assistant Regional Director for FCI. At that time, the Miramar office was downsized to a RAC under the San Diego Field Office. The NIS Southwest Region personnel listing dated March 16, 1992, shows the following for NISRA Miramar: SAC Bruce Smart, Tim Caruth, Joan Otake, Cal Calhoun, J. Weimer, M. Mosell and admin support Delia Jamir.

Chart 13-1 NISRA Miramar

NISRA MIRAMAR (11MM)				
	SRA/SAC	ASRA/ASAC		ADMIN
Jan72-Nov75	D.Foley	K.Sumner	G.Hall, B.Taylor, F.Stilwell, S.Kahl,	L.Covert,
		B.Taylor	J.Pender, S.Schlagel, A.Burroughs,	P.Tomlinson
		A.Deahl	H.Kimball, M.Lingo, Lt S.Deluca	P.Dyck
75-79	D.Wardman	A.Deahl/Stovall	H.Stovall, M.Elliott, R.Sullivan	L.Covert
			K.Oglesbee, S.Deluca, J.Pender	
79-81	W.Lynch	B.Taylor/T.Hicks	H.Stovall, J.Pender, M.Elliott,	
			R.Sullivan	
81-83	M.Whidden	T.Hicks/B.Taylor	J.Pender, M.Elliott, B.Taylor	
			A.Spafford, I.Howard, M.Fox	
Jul83-Nov84	L.Ferrell	G.Helson	M.Fox, I.Howard, A.Spafford,	J.McCarthy,
			B.Yankowski	K.McClone
Nov84-Jul86	R.Rainville	R.Jansen	A.Bedoya, J.Haris, I.Howard, B.Green,	
Jul86-Sep87	E.Simon			
Sep87-Jun90	T.Hicks	W.Focht/	R.Minnoch, J.Perkins, R.Wood	D.Jamir
		D.Valentine		
Jun90-Aug92	B.Smart	S.Wall/T.Carruth	J.Otake, C.Calhoun, J.Weimer, M.Mosell	D.Jamir
11MM became subordinate to the San Diego Field Office upon departure of SA Smart				

14
NISRA MCRD (11MD)/NTC (11NC)/Training Commands (11NC)

For many years, Marine Corps Recruit Depot (MCRD) and Naval Training Center (NTC) were side-by-side facilities in San Diego that provided recruit training for a great number of sailor and marine enlistees. This writer is not aware of the first existence of ONI or NIS onboard either base; however, a 1968 NISO San Diego roster shows three agents assigned to NISRA MCRD (11MD)—Jerome Mooers, James Netzel, and Robert Richardson. By 1974, NISRA MCRD had a SRA—Walt Cleveland, five other agents, and two administrative personnel.

The first office for new agent Wendell Taguchi was NISRA MCRD which also operated a satellite office at NTC. Tag, as he became known, worked at both offices from August 1974 to August 1976 when he transferred to NISRA Naval Station. Tag recalls following ASAC Walt Focht around a lot trying to learn helpful investigative methods and techniques. He also recalls many narcotics possession and use cases, and minor theft of government property investigations—typical caseloads for new agents learning the ropes. Over the years, MCRD and NTC were both scenes of separate NISRAs at either or both locations. And over the years, both offices served as good training grounds for young agents like Tag to learn the business from seasoned professionals. The first SRA for whom Tag worked at MCRD was Walt Cleveland.

In about 1976, By Tardiff reported in as SRA NISRA MCRD and Mike Nagle came in from NISRA Naval Station to lead the agents at NTC. Peter J. Anderson was the MCRD ASRA when Steve Kahl reported in July 1976. Steve Kahl tells us about a USMC 1st Lt who stole three truck loads of telephone poles which had been removed and were destined to be used for obstacle courses at Camp Pendleton. The 1st Lt, who was a recruit series commander, stole them with a friend who had access to a construction truck. He sold them to a garden supply company which cut them up for use in retaining walls. After being convicted at a Special Court Martial on two counts each of theft and conversion, the Lieutenant was sentenced to No Punishment.

NISRAs NTC and San Diego lunch 1977

In July 1977, NTC gained a new ASAC as Ray Larabee checked in to work for SAC Tad Uriu. According to Ray, the workload was heavy in narcotics, strong-arm robbery, and sexual assaults. One memorable case was a strong-arm robbery investigation in which an individual became a person of interest after he was seen during two surveillances. During an initial interview, he made incriminating statements and then was warned as a suspect. At Courts Martial, he was convicted and spent two years in jail. During an appeal, the Court of Military Appeals said NIS should have warned him prior to any initial interview and overturned the conviction. This became a case that changed the way NIS treated suspects.

Doug Stuart reported in as SAC in August 1980, relieving Tad Uriu who had passed away with cancer. Circa 1982 the San Diego Police Department (SDPD) Lieutenant in charge of its Street Narcotics Unit visited Doug Stuart. The unit was aware of rampant drug dealing on the part of taxi drivers in the city and expressed the need for military personnel to pose as drug users and make controlled purchases.

A Military Police Corporal from MCRD was recruited and with command permission was relieved of all USMC duties and "assigned" to 11NC. He was selected not just because of his excellent record, but for his appearance and demeanor which made playing the role of a naïve military member quite believable.

After a few weeks of hailing cabs and making controlled buys under SDPD/NIS surveillance, a major arrest operation was conducted. The SDPD provided about fifty officers and NIS several SAs for the effort. Press people were invited to SDPD HQ. Arrest teams were dispatched and returned piecemeal with arrested taxi driver prisoners. At least forty to fifty cabbies were arrested and all were charged and convicted. During the arrests, many seizures were made including the discovery of an opium poppy farm in one back yard. Local press coverage was extensive and quite favorable.

Those were the days before the military implemented the widespread urine analysis program, and drug use among young military personnel was rampant. It was agreed that the SDPD Street Narcotics Unit and NIS would build on the success of the taxi operation and target civilians dealing drugs to military personnel. The tactics were simple: joint SDPD/NCIS surveillance would be established over a known drug dealer environment. The undercover military person would enter the area and if offered drugs, would make a purchase with recorded funds. The undercover would give a signal of a successful purchase and observing officers/agents would move in and arrest the dealer.

The operation continued for one year primarily on nights and weekends. The same buy funds were used over and over, and one twenty dollar note became quite recognizable for the bloodstains deposited by a dealer foolish enough to resist arrest. At the one year mark, over three hundred dealers had been arrested and all were charged and convicted. Additional undercover sources were selected and trained. Just about every NIS Agent in the San Diego metropolitan area participated in the operation. After about one year, the undercover sources had to be more aggressive and ask suspects if they knew where they could buy some drugs. And often the replies were similar to, "We don't deal to military anymore."

In addition to his innovative approach to combating the narcotics/dangerous drug problems, Doug Stuart also provided new ideas in developing technology that greatly helped NIS in the years ahead. See the chapter on Technology herein.

An August 1980 NISO San Diego roster shows Doug Stuart SAC of NISRA Naval Training Center, Peter Anderson RRA at MCRD, and Bob Barrows RRA at the Naval Hospital. A 1982 NISO San Diego roster shows Doug Stuart SAC of NISRA Training Commands, Peter Anderson RRA at NTC, and Walter Focht RRA at Navy Hospital.

By January 1984, Ken McDonald is listed as SAC of Naval Training Commands, Sam Ferguson is ASAC, Kevin Keating is RRA at the hospital, three other agents are at MCRD, and Peter Anderson is RRA at NTC with three other agents—all supported by two admin personnel. The NISRA is still located at MCRD. In July 1987, Ken McDonald was relieved as SAC by Mike

Bourke but only for a few months. In October, John Davies came in as a new GM-14 SAC. Yes, the same John Davies who became a NIS Plank Owner in 1966 in Long Beach. During his tour as SAC, Davies moved the NISRA office from MCRD to NTC.

John Davies was still in place as SAC of NISRA Training Commands as documented in a March 1992 Southwest Region Personnel Listing. He had Joel Gossett as his ASAC, Brad England as RRA at Ballast Point, Sally Wilson as RRA at Balboa Hospital, eleven other agents, and three administrative positions.

In mid-1992, Ray Larabee relieved John Davies as SAC as the position was downgraded to GM-13. By mid-1994, the San Diego Field Office was established at Naval Station, NISRA Training Commands was disestablished, and Ray Larabee moved over to the Field Office to become a Criminal Squad Leader.

Chart 14-1 NISRA Training Commands

NISRA TRAINING COMMANDS (11NC)				
	SRA/SAC	ASRA/ASAC	AGENTS	ADMIN
unk-68			J.Mooers, J.Netzel, R.Richardson	
unk-Sep74	W.Cleveland	W.Focht	W.Taguchi, M.Frankel, D.Tomaso, L.Link	N.Link,
			M.Nagel (NC), R.Wardman, D.Hershberger	M.Reclau
Sep74-76	D.Hartman	A.Hooser	M.Nagel (NC), S.Spears (HB), M.Evans,	K.Heenan,
			V.McPherson, D.Hershberger, B.Cook,	P.Shosted
			W.Taguchi,D.Driskill, S.Hastings	
76-77	B. Tardiff	M.Nagle	P.Anderson (MD), S.Kahl, Msgt Link	
77-Aug 80	T.Uriu	R.Larabee	P.Anderson (MD) R.Barrows (HB),	B.Baker,
			A.Yates, M.Caul, D.Lucas	N.Gomez
Aug80-Jul83	D.Stuart	T.Boley	P.Anderson (MD), R.Barrows (HB), M.Caul,	
			W.Focht. F.Grim, L.Spinks, R.Grodzicki	
Jul83-Jul87	V.McDonald	S.Ferguson/	P.Anderson (NT), W.Focht(HB), M.Caul,	N.Gomez,
		W.Focht	K.Keating (HB), D.Shaw, T.Smith,	C.Czech
			P.Hurley, J.Noone, L.Spinks	
Jul87-Oct87	M.Bourke	W.Focht/	P.Anderson (NT), K.Keating (HB), P.Hurley,	
		W.Eade	D.Shaw, T.Smith, M.Caul,J.Noone, L.Spinks	
Oct87-Jul92	J.Davies	W.Eade/	F.Wilson (HB), B.England (BL), H.Sherry	C.Mencel,
		J.Gossett	M.Sheahan, F.O'Donnell, C.Click,	P.Anderson
			J.Robertson, W.Herzig, M.Campbell,	W.Lopez
			R.Snyder, K.Rodriguez, R.Rauss, R.Kimler	
Jul92-May94	R.Larabee	J.Gossett	F.Wilson (HB), B.England (BL), H.Sherry,	C.Mencel,
			K.Rodriguez, L.Galicki, C.Clements	P.Anderson

15
Technology/Communications

In the mid-1970s, Doug Stuart served as the Head of the Operations Control Center at NIS Headquarters. In that timeframe, NIS utilized a telecommunications system using Teletype machines which operated as typewriters. Daily, every continental US (CONUS) NISRA put unclassified reports on to a continuous roll of paper tape and transmitted it via the Department of Defense (DoD) AUTOVON network to the NISRO which would upload it to NISHQ. NISHQ used a Univac computer the size of a truck to read distribution codes, sort messages for retransmission and transmit data back to each NISRO which would forward it to each NISRA. This system provided overnight transmission of unclassified data throughout CONUS, but NIS offices outside CONUS had to use US mail or naval message service through Navy communication centers. In time, NIS was dropped from AUTOVON due to overloading of the system. NISHQ realized that a civilian telecommunications system would be too expensive. The only other DoD system was the AUTODIN (Automatic Digital) network which was used for both classified and unclassified data transmission. Each AUTODIN terminal was priced at $25,000.00 per month—far too expensive for NIS. With a little effort, NISHQ realized that its Univac was an AUTODIN terminal which could and did work for NIS worldwide.

While at headquarters, Doug Stuart's suggestion led to the purchase of a Lanier word processor which was integrated into the front office of NISHQ. Since NIS was busy converting from AUTOVON to AUTODIN telecommunications, terminal equipment became an interest item. At this time, there were some new computers that could emulate Teletype machines, one of which was brand name CADO. The IBM PC did not yet exist. The CADO was based upon the newest Western Union fully electronic, Teletype machine with a CRT display and solid state microprocessor. The CRT had twenty-four lines and the processor sixty-four kilobytes of RAM. CADO added two eight-inch floppy disc drives for magnetic storage and word processing software which amounted to one of the very first desk size computers (not desk top). It was priced at $20,000 (1977 dollars)! NIS purchased two CADO machines for "research and development." One of these machines was sent to the Navy Research Lab in San Diego.

In 1980, Doug Stuart became SAC of NISRA Training Commands (11NC) located at NTC San Diego. He soon visited the Navy Lab and found the engineer, Robert Cigletti, who had control of the CADO. Robert had been sent to the CADO programming school and was familiar with the machine but had done nothing of consequence with it since he had received it. Doug told the engineer that he wanted a word processor and a Teletype machine that could produce NIS standard system documents (SSD). Cigletti said all he needed was programming specifications, and Doug developed and gave him the specs.

After the CADO was working, Doug asked NIS Technical Services Division Head John Langager if he could move it to 11NC and he agreed. The machine was installed in the NISRA and performed as needed. The word processing function so improved clerical efficiency that Doug was able to appoint one of the two admin staff as Evidence Custodian freeing an agent of those duties. Before long, another CADO terminal was added for the first inter-office network giving both secretaries access to the system.

The NISO Supervising Agent, Greg Duffy, visited the 11NC office and was most impressed with the CADO. Doug Stuart can still recall the wonder on Duffy's face as the daisy wheel printer flawlessly fired out SSDs at a speed that made typing seem a snail's pace. When the admin staff demonstrated word processing, he was not hesitant to express amazement. Comments such as "You can actually remove a whole paragraph and move it somewhere else?" "You don't have to erase, just type over it?" "You don't have to print it until it is perfect!" Etc. Greg Duffy became a strong proponent of information automation.

That was phase I. Phase II began when CADO released simple data base management software. The software was trade named "Just Ask" and amounted to a few simple commands to process data. By today's standards, it was ridiculously simple. But to a NIS staff that was using 3x5 cards to identify numbers of cases, assigned agent, time since opening/closing or last paper, it was outright amazing. At the time, an example of a NIS case control number was: 01-02-77N11-NCXX-6SNA. The components were as follows: 01-02-77 –date case was opened; N–Service (Navy); 11–NISRO; NC–NISRA; XX–sequential number from CCS assignment log; 6S–category of investigation; NA–Project code.

To use Just Ask, all Doug had to do was to separate the CCN into its component parts. The dates became YYMMDD instead of MMDDYY so a computer could put it in order. He designed two separate files for open and closed cases. The open case file was huge since it had all the case information except closing data, e.g. date, disposition, evidence associated, etc. Just Ask became the first automated case control system (CCS), with which a manager could interrogate the data base and print out ordered lists by any necessary or required criteria. After the system had been up and running for three months and Doug was confident in the system back up procedures, his office staff had a conversion ceremony. The entire shoebox full of 3x5 cards was dumped into the trash.

Phase II was done and Phase III began. NIS had a fully functioning CCS but the paper file system was still arranged by closing date. This system had originally been set up to accommodate requirements of the DoD to purge files based on closing date. If a file is misplaced in a date-based system i.e. wrong year, it can be a monumental effort to find. If a file is misplaced in an alphabet based system, it will still be close to where it should be. It was simple for the CCS to produce a purge list based upon purge criteria. Before long, 11NC had trashed the date filing system and went fully to filing alphabetically. NISRA NTC quit losing stuff!

The Training Commands office soon had a NIS Headquarters inspection. Doug Stuart tried to explain his case management and filing system to incredulous inspectors who could not find anything right about it. To this day, Doug believes the inspectors found it problematical. It worked great but was also a blatant violation of the rules! Doug suspects Greg Duffy absorbed any heat headed towards himself.

In 1983, Stuart was promoted and assigned as SAC NISRA Camp Pendleton. There was a major undercover operation (RipStop) ongoing and a heavy caseload. This NISRA was four times bigger than Training Commands with even larger administrative problems and a high case delinquency rate. The Pendleton 3x5 shoebox was huge and managed almost full time by the ASAC.

Doug soon called John Langager to inquire about the second CADO, and shortly thereafter, it arrived at Camp Pendleton. The Training Commands software was loaded and adapted. Each agent was provided a list of assigned cases by due date. Three months later, the case delinquency rate was zero. The shoebox full of flimsies found the trash can, the ASAC was freed up for other duties and a secretary handled case control.

The ASAC at the time was Toni Perrin who Doug asked to overhaul the evidence control locker system which was fraught with problems. Toni designed a subsystem (still in use by that office thirty years later) that tied the evidence disposal system to the CCS. There were no more problems. All items of evidence were accounted for and properly purged along with the case file. Doug and Toni agreed to hire Tim Jordan as the Evidence Custodian. When he retired some twenty years later, Tim Jordan had a perfect record of evidence accountability, according to Doug Stuart.

Computers began appearing in NIS offices in the early 1980s. Kathy Hampton, Field Office

Support Officer (FOSO) of the Marine Corps West Field Office, began working for NIS in 1984. As Kathy recalls, admin personnel typed documents onto floppy disks using the newly established Peach Text program, reviewed them for content, format, and errors and obtained signoff from the RAC. Other admin support duties included answering telephones, preparing naval messages, getting supervisor signoff, and taking them to the local communication center for transmission. As of the mid 1980s, NIS offices had received some desktop computers for agents, but mostly for admin support. It wasn't until the late 1980s that computers found their way on to desks of all personnel.

Longtime San Diego Special Agent and recent Executive Assistant Director Pacific John Wagner reminds us that when George Bush was president in 1989, there was no commercial internet, computers were used as word processors and fax machines were cutting edge technology. There were no cellular telephones. NIS had hello lines to receive calls from a cooperating witness. The duty agent carried a pager as big as a pack of cigarettes which would tell him to call the security department rather than a beep with call back number. Veteran agents used IBM Selectric typewriters to craft reports. Some used Dictaphones. Younger agents used Winchester disk computers with Peachtext. John Wagner recalls that agents complained about having to learn new commands when NIS changed to WordPerfect around 1991. NIS personnel also had to retype Peachtext documents because there was no way to do file conversions between the programs.

Technology advances have greatly affected NCIS. Again, John Wagner tells us: smart phones which have more capabilities than desktop computers of 2002 have replaced hello lines. Wet film is history and agents no longer wonder if their crime scene photographs are acceptable. Agents conduct consensual intercepts with a global system rather than a suction cup stuck to the back of a telephone handset connected to a tape recorder. Body wires are no longer the size of a deck of playing cards, powered by two 9-volt batteries with antennas that heat up as time passes. Today's devices are more covert with better transmission capabilities, enhancing officer safety and the quality of evidence. A consensual intercept no longer has to be approved by the Navy General Counsel but now has been delegated to the geographic Executive Assistant Directors. The Teletype system that office staff would watch at agent transfer time has disappeared over the years to be replaced by e-mails and Navy and Marine Corps Internet.

16
NISRA North Island (11NI)

The NISRA North Island (11NI) office opened up in August 1968 with GS-12 Ron Bright as its first SRA. Plank Owners were Steven Lane, Arden Norton, David Pare, and Allan Turner according to the NISO personnel roster of 1968. In the next year or so, Lane, Norton, and Pare were replaced by Ted Miller, Carl Sundstrom, Norm Raines, Al Jesse, and Tom Kozlowski. The admin support people, Patsy Claunch and Sharon Wilkason, were also replaced in the early 1970s by Joy Walkley and Penny Shosted. The original 11NI office was located in an old building overlooking San Diego Bay. Between the office and the bay was a snack stand operated by a blind man and a pier at which the USS Chicago would berth. In March 1971, Ron Bright was relieved by Ed Fitzpatrick as SRA, the first GS-13 SRA at this office. Four months later, Joe Brant reported in as the first ASRA of the office.

Since World War II, Naval Air Station (NAS) North Island was a primary West Coast home for aircraft carriers, most of the time, homeport for three carriers. By the early 1970's, NIS realized that the Navy's aircraft carriers and task groups required full time investigative coverage. The Agent Afloat Program was born. Special Agents (SA) were given one year assignments onboard all sixteen or so carriers to provide criminal and counterintelligence investigative support to the carrier itself, embarked Air Wing, and accompanying ships. If the aircraft carrier deployed to Vietnam, Indian Ocean, or Mediterranean Sea, the SA went with it. When the carrier made a port call in Tokyo, Mombasa, or Athens, the SA went with it. Most often, one SA was assigned to a carrier--sometimes, two. It was a demanding job. Much of the time, the Agent Afloat for the San Diego based carriers was selected from the staff at NISRA North Island.

Ted Miller had the pleasure of serving as the Agent Afloat onboard USS Ticonderoga (CVS-14) in 1972. The pleasure came as the ship served as the primary recovery ship for the last manned mission to the moon--Apollo 17, Dec 11-17, 1972, and Astronauts Eugene Cernan, Harrison Schmitt, and Ronald Evans. Ted delights in reliving his experience of being on deck as the recovery vehicle is hoisted onboard Tico.

Allan Larson was assigned to 11NI from September 1972 to July 1975 in several different positions. During this timeframe, a NIS Resident Unit office was established at the Naval Amphibious Base, Coronado, just a few miles south of North Island. Al Larson was selected to be the singular SA assigned until Don Johnson arrived in late 1974. Larson also served as an Agent Afloat for six months while the aircraft carrier was preparing for deployment.

Shootouts with bad guys are not common in the history of NIS. In fact, there have been very few. One legendary shootout occurred in April 1974 in Coronado, CA. Undercover agents (UCA) were attempting to purchase one kilo of cocaine for $29,000 from individuals including two sailors at a street intersection in Coronado. When the suspects arrived at the location, they had guns pointed at the head of a UCA in their vehicle. As he jumped from the suspect's vehicle, all h--- broke loose as gunfire erupted from the vehicle and hidden law enforcement officers including NIS agents Ed Fitzpatrick and Ted Miller. Two of the suspects were injured as various weapons including a sawed-off rifle were recovered at the scene. Neither of the NIS agents were injured.

The September 1974 NISO-wide roster shows the following personnel assigned to 11NI: Ed Fitzpatrick as SRA, ASRA Larry Butler, Al Larson at 11CI, John Consoli, Paul Schubarth, Gerry Strauss, and Allan Sipe, and admin personnel Joy Walkley and Penny Shosted.

The source was a US Navy sailor who was provided $2,400 in marked US currency. He was driven to a location where he was to join up with the suspect and proceed to another known location where the money was to be exchanged for three ounces of black tar heroin. Following the transaction, the source, who we will call Slim, was to walk around the block and meet up law enforcement personnel. The transaction, to be observed by law enforcement, was to end with the suspect in custody and $2,400 back in the hands of the providers. It did not end the way it was planned.

Where did this event occur? New York? New Orleans? Miami? NCIS Los Angeles? Any of the above? When did it happen? 1980s? 1990s? 2000s? 2010s? The answer is none of the above. This drug deal took place in Coronado, California in 1975. At that time, $2,400 was a lot of money to be spent on a drug purchase—even for a Federal Agency like the NIS. It was such a big deal that the Assistant Supervising Agent of NISO San Diego came to North Island to insure the operation succeeded. How did this deal go down? Slim was dropped off near the suspect's barracks onboard NAS North Island by Allan Sipe and another agent. Slim joined up with the suspect—another sailor we will call Joe—and they both walked off base to Joe's car. Slim got the drugs, left the vehicle, gave a prearranged signal, and walked away. NIS Agents and Coronado Police saw the signal, swooped in and arrested Joe. Slim proceeded directly to Sipe's vehicle with three ounces of heroin. One problem. Joe didn't have the money. Slim told us that he had to front the $2,400 to Joe in his barracks room. NIS agents responded to the barracks room. A search warrant was obtained. SAs entered the room and recovered the money. Everybody breathed a sigh of relief as the story ended on a good note.

This writer had the pleasure of serving as the SA onboard USS Constellation (CV-64) in 1976. The carrier was in the process of preparing for overseas deployment—in and out of port for local operations. One highlight occurred after the first at-sea period during which a source provided information about a shipmate who was to engage in selling marijuana from his vehicle parked off base. The writer was able to leave the ship via the Carrier Onboard Delivery (COD) aircraft the morning the ship was entering port, joined up with SA Butler at the office, located the subject's vehicle in a parking lot onboard the base but accessible from off base, and waited for the ship to sound liberty call. A while later, agents observed subject enter his vehicle and apparently conduct a transaction with a shipmate. Agents arrested the subject, recovered marijuana from his vehicle, and pointed out the closest building which housed the NIS office, from which the marijuana transaction was photographed. Besides being a demanding position, the Agent Afloat has always been a sought-after and rewarding position.

In mid-1978, the first women SAs were hired by NIS. One of whom, Tricia Mansel, was assigned to NISRA North Island, according to Ted Miller who had returned to 11NI as ASAC in 1978. Another female agent in this timeframe was Sandy Deluca at NISRA Miramar.

NISRA North Island 1977

Tom Boley reported to 11NI in December 1979 as a senior street agent to SAC Ken Nickel and ASAC Ted Miller. Nickel was very sick and passed away the next Spring. Miller became SAC and Boley became ASAC. In a government property theft case, an 11NI agent, Larry Fuentes, used his ingenuity. Larry had a box made, large enough for a chair and a person, complete with air holes, and positioned strategically in property disposal. Early every morning, Larry got into the box to watch for yard workers "salting" a particular disposal bin with high value materials for a collusive merchant to bid on. Larry worked this job long enough and well enough to collect the video necessary to prosecute.

NISRA North Island 1981

In the fall of 1980, Miller got orders to NIS Headquarters and he departed San Diego in December that year. The next month, Toni Perrin reported in as SAC of 11NI. As of January 1984, Perrin is listed as SAC, Al Larson is ASAC, other agents are K.Burns, T.Darcy, Bob Davis, Bob Fritzsche, Joel Gossett, Tom Hardy, Karl Rodriguez, Robin Parks, Dick Lucas and JoAnn Wickham-Cloonan at North Island, Craig Goodwin at Coronado, and Joy Petty, J.Ferguson, and K. McClone providing admin support. In early 1984, Larry Ferrell who had been Miramar SAC transferred in to be the 11NI SAC.

In July 1984, Ray Larabee was assigned as RA NISRU Coronado. SAC was Ferrell and ASAC was Jack Parkey. Win Kuehl came in as NISO RDO in the same timeframe. Larabee recalls being the lead agent on a brutal homicide case onboard a ship at North Island. Two subjects were convicted at General Courts Martial—one received fifty years confinement and the other ten years as he cooperated with the government.

Two years later in 1986, Jack Parkey moved to a new position at NISO San Diego as Assistant RDO for FCI. Ray Larabee became ASAC 11NI to SAC Larry Ferrell who was followed by Rudy Dees. Dees served until Wayne Clookie became SAC in June 1989.

NISRA North Island 1990

Ed Jex served as Agent Afloat onboard USS Constellation from May 1994 to May 1995. He recalled working 138 cases during his twelve-month assignment. As the San Diego Field Office was created in the 1993-94 timeframe, NISRA North Island SAC position was downgraded to GM-13 with Dave Kuhrt in that role, assisted by Ray Larabee, Mike Shevok, and Matt Butler.

Chart 16-1 NISRA North Island

NISRA NORTH ISLAND (11NI)				
	SRA/SAC	ASRA/ASAC	AGENTS	ADMIN
Aug68-Mar71	R.Bright		S.Lane, A.Norton, D.Pare, A.Turner,	P.Claunch,
			T.Miller, C.Sundstrom, N.Raines, E.Hella,	S.Wilkason
			A.Jesse, T.Kozlowski, G.Brooks	
Mar71--Jul75	E.Fitzpatrick	J.Brant	N.Raines, A. Turner, T.Kozlowski,	E.Walkley,
		L.Butler	C.Sundstrom, T.Miller, A.Larson (CI)	P.Shosted
			P.Shubarth, G.Straus, A. Sipe, J.Consoli	
Jul75--Apr80	K. Nickel	L.Butler	R.Helbock (CI), D.Johnston (CI), Shubarth,	E.Walkley,
		T.Miller	J.Consoli, R. Barelli, H.McLemore,	P.Shosted
			A.Sipe, G.Strauss, D.Wright, A.Yates	
Apr80-Dec80	T.Miller	T.Boley	L.Hamilton (CI), L.Fuentes, K.Rodriguez,	E.Walkley,
			F.Said, R.Fritzche, J.Harris, T.Mansell	S. Rose
Jan81-Jan84	A. Perrin	T.Boley	K.Burns, T.Darcy, R.Davis, R.Fritzsche,	J.Petty,
		D.Larson	J. Wickham-Cloonan, C.Goodwin(CI),	K.McGlone
			K.Rodriguez (CV63), R.Parks (CV-61),	J.Ferguson
			J.Gossett, R.Lucas, T.Hardy	
Jan84-Jul86	L.Ferrell	J.Parkey	R.Larabee (CI), K.Burns (CI), R. Davis,	
			R.Whitehouse, M.Butler,	
Jul86-Jun89	R. Dees	R.Larabee	J.Roberts (FCI), W.Rawlins, D.Wieland,	
			T.Minor, R.Whtehouse, M.Butler, N.Craig	
Jun89-Mar92	W.Clookie	R.Larabee	T.Minor, M.Butler, L.Galicki,	L.Sorrells,
		D.Kuhrt	R.Duwelius (CI), C.Yohn, J.Lee (CV-63)	Y.Schaeffer,
			C.Kisthardt, K.Proffitt-bothFCI, N.Craig	A.Schaffer
			D.Parnell (CV-61),R.Benzel (CV-64)	
North Island office became part of the San Diego Field Office in 1992				

17
NISRA Naval Station, San Diego (11ND)

As of 1968, NIS Resident Agencies in greater San Diego were located at MCRD and NAS North Island. NISRA San Diego, co-located with NISO San Diego on Fordham Street, provided investigative coverage to other metropolitan Navy/Marine Corps installations at Naval Station and NAS Miramar.

According to SA George Reis, who was assigned to the San Diego DIO and NIS Offices from 1959 to the late 1960s, the first NISRA onboard Naval Station was established in about 1970 headed by Wes Howe.

On March 20, 1974, NISRA Naval Station (11ND) was directed to protect the Prince of Wales who was serving at the time as a Lieutenant in the Royal Navy, and his ship, HMS Jupitor, was visiting Naval Station. Tom Clark, a young agent working at 11ND at the time, provided this account. Early in the day, an attempt had been made to kidnap the Prince's sister, Princess Anne, in London. According to Clark, 11ND agents secured the pier where Jupitor was berthed and the gangway to the ship. NISO San Diego personnel arranged for the Prince to be moved to VIP quarters at NAS North Island. This arrangement was maintained until the following morning when Prince Charles returned to his ship which got underway and departed San Diego. Clark said NIS later learned that the London suspect was a mentally deranged loner and there had been no threat to other members of the Royal family.

The February 1975 NISO personnel roster reflects the following for 11ND: SRA Howe, ASRA Mike Nagle, Tom Clark, Dick Lucas, Kent Montgomery, David Moyer, Joe Neal, Bob Robbins, Steve Scott, Tom Williams and admin personnel Jane Petrick and Mary Ziegler.

NISRA Naval Station San Diego—April 1975
(L to R) Tom Williams, Dick Lucas, Steve Scott, Dave Moyer, Jane Petrick, ASAC Mike Nagle, SAC Wes Howe, Mary Ziegler, Joe Neal, Kent Montgomery, Bob Robbins, Tom Clark

NISRA Naval Station 1975

Wendell Taguchi transferred from NISRA MCRD to NISRA Naval Station in August 1976 where he continued for about one year. Tag, as he has always been known, described 11ND as the ultimate training location for new agents with a wide assortment of Crimes against Property (Category 6), Crimes Against Persons (Cat 7), and Sex Crimes (Cat 8) cases including wrongful destruction, breaking and entering, robberies, and narcotics.

In the summer of 1976, Tag and most of the fellow agents who had been hired as GS-7 in the summer of 1974, were preparing to take an examination for promotion to GS-11. Tag recalls the many hours that he and fellow GS-9 agents got together to prepare for this exam. He says that lots of beer and snacks went into this preparation.

Also that summer, NISRAs North Island and Naval Station got together one Saturday at the Navy Athletic Field on Harbor Boulevard to play some slow pitch softball, socialize, and drink some beer. In a doubleheader, the writer pitched one game for the North Island team. Tag came to the plate five times and homered four times. Allan held him to a double the last at bat. He hasn't pitched since.

Grant McIntosh was assigned to 11ND as a brand new untrained GS-7 in August 1978. Over the next two years, he worked with experienced agents to learn but he also carried a heavy caseload (20-25 gen criminal cases) that he was expected to handle on his own. Grant agreed with Tag as he calls 11ND one of the very best offices that a new agent could be assigned because of the wide variety of case work and demands on the agents. When he started at Naval Station, he says there were nine SAs assigned. Grant was transferred in October 1980 as a GS-11 to NISRA Point Loma to become a member of the new fraud squad.

In 1979, 11ND opened an investigation into the theft of 5,000 US Postal Money Orders, a money order imprinter and validation plate, and approximately $15,000.00 in cash. Sometime later, a First Class Postal Clerk was arrested in Texas. A search of his San Diego residence resulted in the recovery of 4,000 money orders, the imprinter, and the validation plate. Much of the credit for the successful resolution of this matter went to Special Agent McIntosh.

A job that sometimes involved many agents was a Protective Service Operation. Grant McIntosh provided the following on Operation Gold Shield, a classic 1981 example. The CNO of the Chile Navy came to the US several times, but this time, for business in Washington, DC, and fun in San Diego. For about one full week, nearly one hundred San Diego agents were occupied 24/7 with providing protective service for this dignitary. This operation was considered necessary due to Chile's seizure of tuna fishing boats, many of which were based in San Diego.

The January 1984 NISO roster reflects the following for 11ND: SAC Don McCoy, ASAC Doug Tomaso, Ralph Blincoe, Rich Cloonan, Jim Garten, Bill Herzig, Mike Hollister, Dan Hurley, Jim Mann, Richard McConnell, P.Phillips, Bob Sanchez, Mark Vallerga, Des Wieland, Lt Jim Eckrich, USN, and Laura Wilson, Lisa Camacho, and Terry Milatz as administrative persons.

Joe Bryant became SAC in August 1985 and served in that position until August 1987 when he was relieved by Harry Stovall. Three ASACs for Criminal matters served under Joe—Doug Tomaso, Bob Helbock, and Harry Rogers. The first ASAC for FCI matters was Allan Larson who filled that position from 1982 to January 1986. Allan Sipe replaced him in July 1986. Joe Brant and the criminal squad agents headed by Jim Mann and then Ray Larabee were located in a wing of the Naval Station Base Security building. The FCI squad was located in a small building in the compound on 32nd street, also occupied by the Officer's Club and the Bachelor's Officer Quarters. The FCI office was established, painted, and occupied by self help efforts of the assigned agents.

One day, a sailor walked into the FCI office and was interviewed by Al Larson. The sailor was from San Salvador and was assigned to the Naval Station. Over the next few weeks, Larson and this person met several times after which Al wrote a detailed report which NIS Headquarters provided to the Central Intelligence Agency. The CIA subsequently presented a certificate to Larson "for his significant assistance to this Agency in its investigation of the 19 June 1985 terrorist attack in San Salvador's Zona Rosa District." The certificate was signed by CIA Director William J. Casey.

NISRA Naval Station 1981

Agents assigned to the criminal squad worked every kind of case imaginable. According to Bob Helbock, the need for Duty Agents to respond to on-base incidents at night was the norm, not the unusual. He added that it was not uncommon for Joe Brant and/or himself to respond to night calls to provide assistance to other agents.

The Base Security/NIS Office building was very old and not well insulated to combat cold weather. It was close to the water where approximately one hundred Navy ships were berthed. Winter winds were frequently uncomfortable and some people in the office supplemented the aged heating system with portable heaters. During a particular cold and blustery morning, Helbock was sitting in his office near the entrance to the NIS Office when he said he heard a shuffling noise in the hallway, approaching from the "bullpen," a term used to describe the office area where a large number of junior agents worked. When Helbock peeked out into the hallway, he saw young agent Matt Butler wearing oversized fluffy slippers in the shape of cats' feet complete with claws. Helbock did not say anything to Butler but chuckled to himself and promised to remember the story for later retelling. Helbock added that Butler had a unique sense of humor and was often the cause of pranks that frequented the office.

While awaiting new office spaces at the Broadway Pier/Navy Supply Center complex, the FCI squad occupied a small building on 32nd Street across from the Navy exchange/ Commissary. One afternoon in mid-1987, occupants of the BOQ next door were seen fleeing the building. As FCI agents responded and began investigating, they learned that a female Navy officer had fired small-arms rounds through the entry door into her quarters and had injured an officer who was trying to talk to her.

As ASAC Allan Sipe notified SAC Stovall, the remaining FCI agents responded to secure the building and hasten evacuation. SA Ron Snyder, a trained hostage negotiator, began attempting to communicate with the female officer. Shortly, the FCI Office became the Command Center as SAC Harry Stovall and the Naval Station Commanding Officer (NAVSTA CO) arrived along with others. Inside the BOQ, nothing was happening. It was empty of residents and communication had not been established with the female officer. Minutes turned into hours. In the evening as it became apparent that the situation had become a stalemate, it was suggested that contact be effected with swat teams to determine possible courses of action.

NISRA Naval Station San Diego 1987

Contact was made with leaders of the San Diego Police Department (SDPD) and Federal Bureau of Investigation (FBI) swat teams. Ultimately with the concurrence of the NAVSTA CO, the SDPD team's offer to respond to provide advice and action if necessary was accepted. The SDPD team arrived with a trained canine and began preparing for entry in another room of the BOQ. As of late evening with no communications with the female officer for hours, the CO authorized flashbang canisters be fired into her BOQ room. After another hour or so, the CO authorized swat team entry into her room. As the SDPD team made entry into her bedroom, the female officer fired small arm rounds, one of which hit one of the officers in his knee. She was immediately subdued and arrested. The officer suffered a minor wound. The Navy Officer was subsequently dispatched to a Navy Hospital for treatment.

On the morning of March 10, 1989, a pipe bomb exploded and set fire to a minivan on a busy street near the University Towne Center shopping mall in San Diego. The vehicle driver, Sharon Rogers, escaped uninjured as she sat stopped at a red light. The van was registered in the name of her husband, Will Rogers III, who was a US Naval Officer, most notable as the captain of the cruiser USS Vincennes, which shot down Iran Air Flight 655 in the Persian Gulf nine months earlier.

NIS, FBI, and SDPD responded to the crime scene. Thus began an investigation that involved multiple agencies and hour after hour of painstaking fact-finding. The initial motivation was thought to be international terrorism in reaction to the Persian Gulf incident. A command center, staffed with FBI and NIS agents, directed the extensive investigation. NIS provided around the clock personal security detail to Will Rogers. Both agencies joined forces in conducting interviews and other investigative inquiries.

Five months later, the Associated Press reported that the FBI had shifted focus away from terrorism towards the possibility of someone with a personal vendetta against Capt. Rogers. On February 17, 1993, the case was featured on the TV show *Unsolved Mysteries*, but no additional information was uncovered. The bombing remains an unsolved case.

Protective Service Details are generally time-consuming events that very seldom offer levity. One that did happened in early October 1989, and is reported by Special Agent Ed Jex. Dmitri Yazov, the Soviet Union Minister of Defense, paid a one-day visit to San Diego when he toured Camp Pendleton and Naval Station San Diego. That evening he and his entourage stayed at the Hotel Del Coronado.

NIS provided a PSD throughout the visit. Ed Jex was on the FCI Squad at NISRA Naval Station at the time, and he was tasked to monitor the visit and the Minister's group for anything of counterintelligence value. He worked closely with the agents from the PSD since they had the closest access.

The evening the visitors stayed at the hotel, Ed went to the PSD "control room" at the hotel. It was a regular room on the same floor where the visitors were housed. The bed was removed and a table and chairs put in place. Like any control room, it was full of communications equipment and other gear associated with the detail. As Ed recalls, there were three NIS agents plus himself and three Soviet security detail men in the room. Ed didn't know which Soviet agency they were from but thought they were probably GRU or KGB. So there they all were, sitting in a room looking at each other. There was no TV or other distraction. None of the NIS guys spoke Russian, and the Russians pretended they didn't speak English.

After about fifteen minutes, it was getting pretty warm in the room, and one of the NIS agents took off his suit coat. On his hip was his NIS issued Ruger .357 revolver. One of the Russians pointed to it, and made a gesture like "can I see that?" So the agent thought for a moment, then shrugged, slowly unholstered the weapon, emptied out the rounds, and handed it to the Russian. He smiled, looked it over, and showed it to his comrades. Then he reached inside his coat and drew a Torkarev pistol from a shoulder holster, unloaded it, and handed to the NIS guy. They all checked out his piece. Then one of the Russians opened up a large briefcase and showed off a cut-down AK-47 style weapon. So of course a NIS guy uncased one of their UZI submachine guns and showed it to the Russians. By then, everyone was smiling, and suddenly it seemed all the Russians remembered how to speak English. "I'll show you my gun if you show me yours" was the brand of Glasnost employed that evening by these cold warriors.

History was made in San Diego on July 31, 1990 with the first ever visit to the port by three ships of the USSR Navy. The Pacific Fleet Commander-in-Chief was here to host his counterpart, the Commander of the Soviet Pacific Fleet. As you can imagine, the visitors were treated to a full schedule of events during the five day visit to Naval Station.

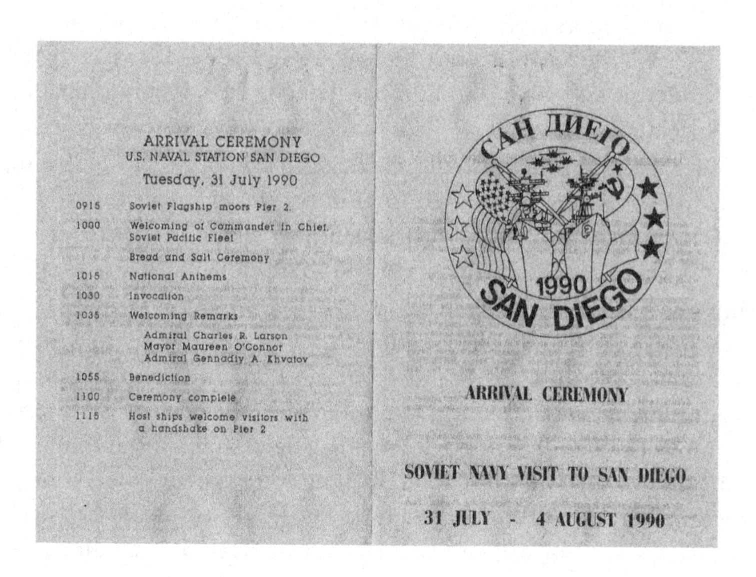

ARRIVAL CEREMONY
U.S. NAVAL STATION SAN DIEGO
Tuesday, 31 July 1990

0915	Soviet Flagship moors Pier 2.
1000	Welcoming of Commander in Chief, Soviet Pacific Fleet
	Bread and Salt Ceremony
1015	National Anthems
1030	Invocation
1035	Welcoming Remarks Admiral Charles R. Larson Mayor Maureen O'Connor Admiral Gennadiy A. Khvatov
1055	Benediction
1100	Ceremony complete
1115	Host ships welcome visitors with a handshake on Pier 2

САН ДИЕГО
1990
SAN DIEGO

ARRIVAL CEREMONY

SOVIET NAVY VISIT TO SAN DIEGO

31 JULY - 4 AUGUST 1990

Soviet Navy visit

By the early 1990s, NISRA Naval Station had been located in a wing of the base security building for many years and was occupied by about twenty-five agents and six support personnel. Since the NISRA needed more space to operate, SAC Harry Stovall wanted to move; however, the only available space was an unoccupied barracks. Harry developed a concept of unifying all the local San Diego NISRAs into an organization similar to the FBI Field Office with a GM-15 SAC, discussed and received approval from RDO Dennis Usrey, and submitted the ideas to NISHQ to obtain funding. They were told to proceed with self help and provided only $100 thousand. SA Richard Grodzicki became project manager. The SEABEES became the construction force. Time became the enemy. But work proceeded.

In addition to specific items discussed herein, other memories of Harry Stovall during his tenure as 11ND SAC: the first assignment of a NIS Special Agent to the San Diego Narcotics Task Force—a group of federal, state, and local agency representatives co-located with DEA and charged with major narcotics investigations—the oldest NTF in the US; NIS participation in the first Light the Night SDPD-sponsored night run from downtown to Balboa Park; many enjoyable hours spent with office-mates during lunches and social hours at the NAVSTA Main Brace club; office participation in annual law enforcement softball tournaments; the co-location of the NIS Forensic Laboratory in the new NIS office space.

The March 1992 NISO personnel roster lists the following for 11ND: SAC Stovall, Criminal ASAC Art Hymons, FCI ASAC Robin Parks, fourteen additional agents, one naval officer, and six support personnel.

In July 1992, Harry Stovall was relieved as SAC 11ND by John Marquette who continued overseeing the new office construction. Harry Stovall retired. Grant McIntosh had served as ASAC for criminal matters under Stovall and he continued such under Marquette. In January 1994, the construction was completed. It was during this timeframe that 11ND along with the RFL, CEF, and other elements moved from the old Naval Base Security Building across the street to the new building. In time, RDO Frank Melia relocated to the new office to become SAC of the new San Diego Field Office (SDFO). Grant McIntosh and Ray Larabee then headed criminal squads that covered all of San Diego County. See a following chapter on the San Diego Field Office.

Chart 17-1 NISRA Naval Station

NISRA NAVAL STATION (11ND)				
	SRA/SAC	ASRA/ASAC	OTHER AGENTS	ADMIN
1970-Jul75	W.Howe	M.Nagel	J.Byrd, T.Clark. K.Montgomery	J.Petrick,
			D.Moyer, J.Neal, R.Robbins, T.Williams	M.Ziegler
Jul75-78	E.Johnson	R.Curtis	W.Taguchi, R.Dempsey, E.Simon, L.Lawing,	M.Ziegler,
			G.Afflick, M.Evans, R.Robins, T.Clark,	L.Melia
			G.McIntosh, K.Montgomery	
78-80	W.McGinnis	F.Melia	G.McIntosh, D.Johnson, R.King, L.Skinner,	
			V.Telles, J.Henderson, H.McLemore	
			W.Turner	
80-82	L.Butterfield	K.MacDonald	K.Bray, R.Sanchez, M.Hollister, D.Eoff	L.Camacho,
			R.Cloonan, D.Hurley, P.McMillan, F.Grim,	M.Ziegler
			R.Benjamin, R.Grodzicki, M.Butler,	S.Berg
			R.Blincoe, M.Shanley, M.Vallerga	
			P.Dickenson, R.Larabee, W.Herzig	
82-85	D.McCoy	D.Tomaso	R.Blincoe, R. Cloonan, J.Garten, W.Herzig,	L.Wilson,
			D.Hurley, J.Mann, R.McConnell, P.Phillips,	E.Camacho
			M.Vallerga, D.Wieland, LT J.Eckrich	S.Berg
			M.Hollister, R.Sanchez	T.Milatz
Aug85-Jul87	J.Brant	R.Helbock-Crim	R.Larabee, W.Eade, M.Haley, M.Acevedo,	L.Wilson,
		H.Rogers-Crim	P.Dickenson, M.Butler, L.Hamilton, K.Shultz,	E.Camacho
			R.Bolden, K.Frestel, J.Deguzman	S.Berg
		A.Larson/	R.Snyder, E.Jex, E.Boyd, R.Parks, T.Smith,	K.Hammonds
		A.Sipe-FCI	L.Miura, M.Elliott, J.McDougal	
Jul87-Jul92	H.Stovall	H.Rogers-Crim	R.Grodzicki, W.Herzig, C.Warmuth, J.Gossett,	L.Wilson,
		A.Hymons-Crim	M.Devine, R.Flanders, L.Clements, K.Hayes,	D.Milton,
			L.Clements, C.Click, B.England, D.Mylius,	J.Domingo,
			W.Eade, R.Dorenbush, B.Nakasone, R.Keen	P.Anderson,
			D.Robertson, J.Robertson, P.Dickenson,	D.Schneiders
			S.Zimmer, J.Kilnap, R.Grodzicki, C.Yohn	P.Joons, S.Berg
		A.Sipe/	M.Elliott, E.Jex, J.MacNeil, R.McFetridge,	E. Camacho,
		R.Parks-FCI	J.McDougal, E.Boyd, E.Sweeney, R .Clifford,	C.Potts
			J.Heinselman, D.Floto	
Jul92-Jul94	J.Marquette	G.McIntosh/	M.Haley, W.Herzig, M.Devine, L.Clements,	D.Milton,
		R.Larabee	B.Nakasone, H.Sherry, C.Schanz, M.Sweeney	S.Berg
			B.England, M.Butler, R.Bolden, R.Dorenbush	
			C.Kisthardt, J.Deguzman, D.Heintz, J.Kohler	
		C.Link-FCI	E.Jex, K.Proffitt, J.Heinselman, D.Floto	

18
Regional Forensic Laboratory

The following information was provided by Brandon Armstrong who obtained some of it from Special Agent Bruce Given, former head of the Forensic Sciences Division (Code 0026A), NIS Headquarters, and some from his own experiences.

During the 1970's, illicit drug use in the Armed Forces was widespread and causing very serious personnel problems. Early approaches to correcting the drug use in the Department of Navy included specific emphasis on identifying traffickers and instituting diligent enforcement of street drug use and possession policies.

On 20 August 1980 in response to the need for timely analysis of suspected substances and routine court evidence presentations, the Chief of Naval Operations authorized the establishment and funding of NIS Drug Identification Laboratories in three locations including San Diego, California. The mission of these laboratories was to "provide drug identification laboratory assistance and associated court testimony to the entire Navy/Marine Corps law enforcement community in a given geographic area." A fourth laboratory was later added.

After locating suitable building spaces and arranging for the transfer of these facilities to NIS control, The NIS San Diego Regional Forensic Laboratory (RFL) came "on-line" 21 December 1982 with the late Dottie Boyer Director. The first staffing consisted of a Senior Chemist (Director), two chemists, one Evidence Custodian, and one secretary.

Alike the other RFLs, the lab was equipped with a Beckman 4250 Infrared spectrum analyzer controlled by a Digital MINC computer, a Beckman DU-8 UV/VIS Spectrophotometer and a Perkin Elmer Sigma 300 Gas Chromatograph.

As the NISRFLs became more thoroughly integrated in the general NIS mission, it became obvious to both investigators and scientists that other law enforcement objectives could be facilitated. The analysis of arson evidence and a latent fingerprints were initiated in 1986. Questioned Document examinations became another service of the RFLs in 1988. The Forensic Sciences Division of the NISHQ Technical Services Department also devoted a significant portion of time and resources to basic and applied research resulting in several noteworthy investigative aids for both NIS personnel and the field of forensic sciences in general. Special Agent Given developed the first standard, agency-wide drug kit for routine field tests. Another widely used development was the rape evidence collection kit which provided the investigator with necessary equipment for tests used by laboratories in those pre-DNA days. Perhaps the greatest value of this kit was the inclusion of an exhaustive protocol, developed through close liaison with the Armed Forces Institute of Pathology, for use by the examining physician, especially one not familiar with the requirements of forensic medicine. Another seldom used, but potentially valuable kit was used to "tag" petroleum products needed by the investigator to document that a particular batch of gasoline was stolen from a naval activity. Involved in the handling of nearly all evidentiary material was the Evidence Custody Document, tamper-proof evidence seals, and NIS Evidence Log, all developed by Code 0026A.

Dottie Boyer served as Director until her retirement in December 1988. Brandon Armstrong assumed duties as Lab Director in January 1989 after retiring as Director of the San Diego Sherriff's Department Crime Lab. During Brandon's time as RFL Director, the Consolidated Evidence Facility (CEF) was attached to the Lab for supervision and oversight. The San Diego RFL ultimately had positions for two fingerprint specialists, two forensic chemists, two document examiners, two evidence custodians, and a secretary.

A San Diego Field Office roster dated 29August 1995 shows Brandon Armstrong and eight other laboratory personnel. Brandon served as Director until Jan. 2001. He was followed by San Diego Forensic Chemist Dawn Sorenson as Director. In the Fall of 2005, Armstrong says, Dawn Sorenson transferred to NCIS Headquarters 0026. She was replaced at the San Diego RFL by the Fingerprint Examiner James Lawson. According to Brandon, Dawn Sorenson was tasked with closure of the NCIS Laboratory System including all four labs by May 2006. In San Diego, the Evidence Facility and its staff were transferred to the Southwest Field Office. A Document Examiner was transferred to the Technical Unit. Another employee became a Crime Scene Specialist. Jim Lawson retired. And that was the end of twenty-four years of professional and accessible criminal evidence processing and analysis available to San Diego area NCIS agents.

San Diego Regional Forensic Lab
Front-Peddie Rousakis
Middle-Brandon Armstrong, Dawn Sorenson, Bill Corson, Max Stayrook
Back-Robert Blackledge, Jerilyn Hammond, James Lawson

19
San Diego Field Office (SDFO)/Southwest Field Office (SWFO)

The San Diego Field Office (SDFO) began to take shape in 1994. GS-15 John Marquette had been the SAC of the Naval Station Office (11ND) since July 1992, and had relocated that office into the refurbished new office. The ceremonial Ribbon Cutting for the new Field Office was in January 1994 with NCIS Director Roy Nedrow assisted by SAC John Marquette doing the honors. At that time, Frank Melia was still RDO of NISO San Diego which remained in the Federal Building.

Field Office Opening Ceremony

In mid-1994, Melia relocated to the Naval Station office and became the Field Office SAC with Marquette becoming the Deputy SAC or DSAC. Vince Giame came down from Camp Pendleton to become the ASAC for Criminal Investigations, Russ Porter became ASAC for Fraud and Cliff Link, the ASAC for FCI. Some Special Agents previously assigned at other NISRAs in the greater San Diego area remained in place to provide stability during this transition period.

In December 1995, John Marquette retired and Giame elevated to DSAC with Wayne Clookie becoming the ASAC for Criminal matters. The Criminal Investigation group became so large that it required two Squad Leaders—Ray Larabee and Mike Bourke came in from Training Commands and the NISO to fill those roles.

A San Diego Field Office roster dated August 1995 shows the following: SAC Melia, DSAC Marquette, ASACs Clookie, Kahl, and Link, fifty-three other Special Agents and one USN SAUSA in San Diego; twenty agents and one USMC Officer SAUSA at Camp Pendleton; twenty administrative support; two computer systems technicians; six budget/finance people; four polygraphers; five SAs and two admin persons in Yuma; nine people at Regional Forensic Laboratory; eight people at the Law Enforcement and Physical Security Assistance Team; and nine people at the Mobile Training Team.

In 1996 the SDFO became the Southwest Field Office (SWFO). That year, it partnered with San Diego Police Department to form the first federal/local law enforcement Emergency Negotiations Team (ENT) in the US. Later, the FBI joined. Now, there are three joint teams each composed of a SDPD Detective Sergeant, five SDPD Detectives, and three Special Agents each from the FBI and NCIS. Whenever there is a call, twelve negotiators respond to ensure public safety and try to save lives. The ENT routinely responds to barricaded suspect/hostage incidents, "suicides in progress" (jumpers, persons armed and threatening suicide, etc), and all SWAT incidents in San Diego city. The team also responds to similar incidents onboard military and other federal property in the area. Since 1996, ENT has responded to two or three incidents per month--nearly thirty percent of which involve active-duty or prior military personnel, dependents, and DOD affiliated persons or contractors. NCIS participation allows immediate access to military records and assets. Assigned personnel are graduates of a forty-five hour negotiations course run locally by the FBI. Many ENT members have advanced training and all are required to undergo annual refresher training. This remains the only team of its kind in the United States.

San Diego Field Office 1996

From October 1997 to March 2002, GS-14 Ron Larson was assigned as the ASAC for FCI of the SWFO. Through the initial seven months of this assignment, Larson also served as the FCI ASAC in San Francisco. Larson served under three SACs--Cliff Simmen, Chuck Briant, and John Cooper--and supervised a FCI Squad that numbered over twenty-five personnel. His duties included administrative, planning, and budget matters. Both the USS Cole and 9/11 terrorist attacks occurred during Larson's assignment as ASAC FCI. The 9/11 attacks specifically changed the entire complexion and focus of the SDFO and the FCI Program. The typical FCI program just about disappeared and counterterrorism became the priority. As the 9/11 attacks were unfolding, essentially the entire SDFO agent staff began working for Larson. The Senior Street Agents (SSA) from both the Criminal and FCI programs and Larson worked together to produce a very aggressive CT/FCI Plan following the 9/11 attack. The plan was validated by NCIS Headquarters and immediately implemented throughout the Southwest Region.

Jewel Seawood was assigned as ASAC of the Crim Squad as a GS-14 from December 2001 to March 2004. She recalls the average case load as about fifteen per agent with crimes against persons and crimes against property the dominant categories. According to Jewel, the most significant case was a homicide of a US Navyman in Tijuana, Mexico in June 2002. He was stabbed during a fight at a nightclub. All involved in the incident were US citizens. In addition to NCIS, the investigation ultimately involved the FBI, US Marshals Service, US State Department, and the Government of Mexico. A suspect and his friends were identified. The subject confessed. The subject was arrested in June 2011 pursuant to an official request by the government of Mexico for his arrest and extradition on charges of aggravated homicide. The subject's arrest concluded a nine year investigation involving substantial diplomatic efforts, complex international issues, and extensive legal proceedings. The subject was ordered extradited to Mexico in November 2011. In the end, said Seawood, the US Attorney and Government of Mexico declined to prosecute and the subject was released from custody.

From the days of the first female SAs in 1978 through the 1980s and 1990s, women agents came onboard NIS and NCIS in increasing numbers. In 2003, Erika Mariner started working at the SWFO where about eleven other women SAs were assigned. In her first year, Erika said she moved through four or five separate squad assignments including undercover operations. This was training that not all women SAs were required to undertake, yet it served to prepare her for different facets of the job that she has carried forth. Erika returned to the SWFO in July 2014 where she has been working on the extensive Glenn Defense Marine Asia contractor bribery investigation.

Since Frank Melia completed his tour as the first San Diego or later Southwest Field Office (SWFO) SAC, there have been seven Special Agents in Charge in the twenty-three year history of this office. The below chart lists this sequence and timeframes of assignments. From June 2014 to the present, the SAC has been Gunnar Newquest. He is assisted by five managers, about twelve SSAs, approximately one hundred Special Agents, and seventeen or so administrative and support personnel who are organized into the Field Office itself and four remote NCIS Resident Agencies. The SWFO covers the area encompassed by California, Nevada, Utah, Colorado, Arizona, New Mexico, and most of Texas other than that covered by the Marine Corps West Field Office (MCWFO).

Chart 19-1 San Diego Field Office/Southwest Field Office

SAN DIEGO FIELD OFFICE				
	SAC	ASAC	Other Agents	Admin
Dec94-	F.Melia	Crim V.Giame/	C.Braatz, R.Braatz, K.Bray, J.Gossett	L.Wilson,
May97-	DSAC	W.Clookie	V.Cernosek, J.Cooper, P.Corcoran,	C.Mencel
	J.Marquette	FCI C. Link	M.Giordani, W.Herzig, B.Smart, J.Lee,	D.Schneiders,
		Fraud S.Kahl/	R.Stapels, M.Thompkins, D.Nelson,	D.Milton,
		R.Porter	T.Buongervino, J.DelaCruz, P.Lim,	S.Smith, K.Smith
			M.Singleton, M.Sweeney, J.Moss	E.Camacho,
			A.Bedoya, M.Chapman (Poly)	P.Anderson,
May97-	C.Simmen	Crim W.Clookie	E.Sweeney, K.Fabrizio, K.Low, D.Few	D.Austin--budget
Jan99-	DSAC	FCI C.Link/R.Larson	M.Shanley, M.Dotter, R.Grodzicki,	M.Katayonis-Anal
	V.Giami	Fraud R.Porter	J.Hermann, C.Calimer, J.Grant,	V.Homfeld-RCFL
			R.Parks, J.Heinselman, R.Rodriguez,	
			C.Caballero, A.Burkhardt, C.Cherer	
			R.Kimler, N.Newquist, J.Otake,	
			J.Lee, T.Piper, T.Minor, D.Floto	
Jan99-	C.Briant	Crim J.Seiber	A.Bedoya, J.Deguzman, M.Giordani,	
Mar00-	DSAC	FCI R.Larson	D.Hershberger, P.Lim, K.Low,	
	C.Link	Fraud R.Porter	T.Minor, E.Schmidt, K.Thomas,	
			K.McSwiggen, R.Staples, T.Bovee	
Mar00-	J.Cooper	Crim J.Seawood	SSAs-D.Johnson, J.Lee, S.Simon	C.Mencel,
06	DSAC	FCI R.Larson/	M.Thompson, M.Sweeney, E.Jex	P.Anderson,
	W.Clookie	B.Dolinka		L.Camacho
		Fraud R.Porter		M.Crumbley
06-	P.Hughes	Crim C.Warmuth/		C.Mencel
09		B.Curley		V.Homfeld
		FCI K.Murphy		
		CT J.Moeller/		
09-	J.Morrow	North T.Buongervino	SSAs-C.Bishop, M.Campbell, E.Jones,	D.Austin,
Mar12-		Crim B.Curley	S.Geyer, M.Giordani, W.Halloran,	C.Mencel
		FCI M.Evans	C.Humenansky, E.Jex, M.Clement	
May14-		CT C.Warmuth	M.Knox, K.Kyser, T. Larson (CK),	C.Mencel
			D.Massey (LA), A.Murphy, J.Nocon,	V.Homfeld
Mar12-	S.Simon			
May14-				
Jun14-	G.Newquist	North T.Buongervino	SSAs-P.Rabin, M.Campbell, P.Griffith,	C.Mencel,
Present		Crim E.Denion	M.Starostka, D.Salazar, C.Peterson,	R.Solomon
		CT S.Roehrick	J.Nocon,A.Tedia,M.Ashton,J.Mariner	V.Homfeld
		SIO S.Crawford		

20
Technical Services/Polygraph Program

Bob Steele and George Reis are believed to be the first polygraphers assigned to the San Diego area, both employed at the DIO in the early 1960s. From that timeframe until now, the polygraph program has been a vital part of the NIS/NCIS resources. For many years, one polygrapher was assigned to the staff of NISO San Diego. He would travel throughout the San Diego Region administering technical examinations for resolutions of both counterintelligence and criminal investigative matters. Tommy Williams served in this position in the mid-1970s, Dave Galanti in the late 1970s-early 1980s, and Jim Pender and Terry Davidson in the mid-1980s. Joe Naylor was assigned as the Western Polygraph Coordinator in the late 1980s-early 1990s under RDOs Win Kuehl, Dennis Usrey, and Frank Melia. As such, he reviewed polygraph examinations and supervised the polygraph program in San Diego, San Francisco, Bremerton, WA, Alaska, Japan and the Philippines.

By the 1990s, the demand for polygraph services had grown and multiple examiners were needed in NCIS San Diego, necessitating creation of a polygraph squad emplaced for several years in Mission Valley. With creation of the Field Offices in San Diego and Camp Pendleton in the 1990s/early 2000s, polygraph units comprised of several examiners and admin support became integrated elements at both locations. The March 1992 NIS Southwest Region Personnel Listing shows the following assigned to the Polygraph Unit: SAC Pat Hurt, Debbie Baker, J.Atkinson, J.Pelton, R. Bieler and support person Carloyn Tanzi. A March 2010 NCIS Marine Corps West Field Office roster shows five polygraph examiners and one admin person.

The first designated Technical Service agent assigned to NISO San Diego is believed to be Brian Greene who is known to have served here in the late 1970s-mid1980s. He was followed by Joe Stephens in the mid to late 1980s.

Jack Marine was assigned to the San Diego Technical Services Department from 1988 to 1996, generally with one other person. He worked out of the Federal Building NISRO until early 1989 when TSD moved to Miramar and two years later to Naval Training Center. Jack said he supported the Southwest and Northwest Regional Offices until a TSD SA was assigned to Seattle. Work included general technical support, installing cameras and listening devices, and support of surveillance ops for fraud and general criminal investigations as well as FCI operations.

21
Executive Assistant Director Pacific (EADPAC)

The Executive Assistant Director for Pacific Operations (EADPAC) position was established in the mid-2000s to oversee NCIS activities in virtually one/half of the world. The EADPAC responsibilities include the management and operational direction of seven NCIS field offices, one Security Training Assistance and Assessment Team, and numerous subordinate elements located throughout the northwestern, southwestern, and central United States, Hawaii, the Far East, Southwest Asia, Middle East, and aboard carrier strike groups and expeditionary strike groups.

The first person to be assigned to the EADPAC position was Ernie Simon who initially worked out of an office at Naval Station San Diego but moved to facilities in Pearl Harbor, Hawaii. He was followed by Assistant Directors Mark Ridley, Mark Clookie, Sam Worth, and John McCoy. Under John McCoy, the EADPAC office relocated to San Diego

John Wagner served in this assignment from December 2012 to April 2015 when he retired. He says his office duties included ensuring quality control of investigations and operations, maintaining strategic engagement with flag and general officers in the PACOM and NORTHPACOM Areas of Responsibility, contact with NCIS Headquarters executives, conducting office visits and inspections of Field Offices. Major commands serviced by these Field Offices included Commander in Chief, Pacific; Commander Pacific Fleet; Commander Marine Forces Pacific; Commander Third Marine Expeditionary Force; Commander Third Fleet; Commander 7the Fleet; Commander Naval Forces Japan; Commander Naval Forces Korea; Commander First Marine Expeditionary Force; Commander First Marine Division; Chief of the Naval Reserve in the Southwest, Northwest and Hawaii; and Commander Naval Training Command Great Lakes.

Following John Wagner's retirement, Charles Warmuth filled the position of EADPAC until the selection of Andrew Snowdon who assumed the position in the Spring of 2016.

Chart 21-1 EADPAC

EADPAC				
DATES	DIRECTOR	LOCATION	STAFF	ADMIN
2005-Jul06	E.Simon	NAVSTA, S. Diego		
Jul06-Aug07	M.Ridley	Pearl Harbor, HI		
Oct07-Apr09	M.Clookie	Pearl Harbor, HI		
Apr09-Aug10	S.Worth	Pearl Harbor, HI		
Sep10-Nov12	J.McCoy	Pt Loma, S.Diego		
Dec12-Apr15	J.Wagner	Pt Loma, S.Diego	G.Newquist, J.Mashny,	J.Gibson
			C.Low, R.Williams, R.Luna,	
			A.Kidd. M.Timmons,	
			J.Donahue, J.Lynn, T.Hawkes	
May15-Mar16	C.Warmuth	Pt Loma, S.Diego		
Jan16-present	A.Snowdon	Pt Loma, S.Diego		

22
NISRA Yuma (11YU)

NISRA Yuma opened sometime between 1968 and 1974 onboard the Marine Corps Air Station (MCAS), Yuma, Arizona. As of September 1974, Stan Fugii was the SAC, Vern McDonald was the only other agent, and Celestina Rojas was their secretary.

Lou Sanchez has told the writer that he was the very first Mexican-American Special Agent hired by NIS in October 1967. In about August 1976, Sanchez was assigned to a one-man office at NISRU El Centro, CA, subordinate to NISRA Yuma. Sanchez also served as ASAC and SAC of NISRA Yuma. Sanchez became the first Hispanic to retire as a Special Agent from NCIS in 1994.

In July 1976, Michael B. Jones reported in to relieve Stan Fugii who had already departed for Okinawa, Japan. Vern McDonald was ASAC. Lou Sanchez was in El Centro. Paul Valentine was an onboard agent and Marine GySgt Jim Daughtey was also assigned.

Two years later, Mike Jones was replaced as SAC by Fred Seehorn as that position was upgraded to GS-13. Also in 1978, Lou Sanchez closed the El Centro office and became ASAC to Seehorn.

In 1980, Seehorn departed, Sanchez became SAC, and McDonald served as ASAC. In 1983, Sanchez transferred to NISRA Washington, DC and McDonald was promoted to replace him.

Ed Jex was assigned to NISRA Yuma from April 1983 to August 1985. He began as a GS-7 and left as a GS-11. The NIS office was located in the Military Police Building at the MCAS, Yuma. The typical workload was twenty to twenty-five cases per agent covering such crimes as theft of government property, narcotics, aggravated assaults, sex crimes, and insufficient fund or fraudulent check writing. A significant case involved LSD usage by the base Air Traffic Controllers. One of them was the supplier-dealer and many were users. They were all arrested. The USMC had to arrange to send a dozen controllers from MCAS El Toro, Camp Pendleton, and Cherry Point, North Carolina, to Yuma for months to cover the loss of personnel. Jex recalled the office frequently held Friday afternoon "meetings" at the Sky Chief Lounge.

As of January 1984, the NISO San Diego roster showed McDonald as SAC, Frank Feiger as SSA, Ed Jex and Rick Wilson as GS-7 agents, and Dorothy Heyl as the admin person.

Vern McDonald is believed to have served as SAC at 11YU until he was relieved by Mark Pendell in March 1992. The Southwest Region Personnel Listing of March 1992 shows the following at 11YU: SAC Pendell, ASAC Bernie Yankosky, E.Chapman, Dan Mylius, J.Graham, SSGT G.Moreno, admin support A.Adams and S.Brassard and Special Agents D.Geiger and J.Karshner at NISRU El Paso. In 2001, NISRA Yuma became a part of the Marine Corps West Field Office.

Chart 22-1 NISRA Yuma

NISRA YUMA (11YU)				
	SRA/SAC	ASRA/ASAC	AGENTS	ADMIN
Sep74-Jun76	S.Fujii		V.McDonald, L Sanchez (EC)	C.Rojas
Jul76-Aug78	M.Jones	V.McDonald	L.Sanchez (EC), P.Valentine	Sally
			Gysgt J. Daughtey, Gysgt,	
Aug78-Aug80	F.Seehorn	L.Sanchez	P.Peters, P.Valentine, J.Daughtey USMC	
Aug80-Sep83	L.Sanchez	V.McDonald	E.Jex, F.Feiger, R.Vaisa, J.Kirkpatrick USMC	D.Heyl
Oct83-Mar92	V.McDonald		F.Feiger, E.Jex, R. Wilson	D.Heyl
Mar92-Mar94	M.Pendell	B.Yankowsky	E.Chapman, J.Graham, Ssgt G.Moreno	A.Adams,
			D.Mylius, D.Geiger (EP), J.Karshner (EP)	S.Brassard
			K.Murphy	
Mar94-Jun96	B.Yankosky		E.Chapman, A.Hatch, J.Cedar, K.Murphy	R.McPherson,

23
Glossary

ARDO	Assistant Regional Director for Operations
ASAC	Assistant Special Agent in Charge
ASRA	Assistant Senior Resident Agent
BI	Background Investigation. Same as PSI.
BRAC	Base Realignment and Closure Commission
DIO	District Intelligence Office
DON	Department of the Navy
DRDO	Deputy Regional Director for Operations
FCI	Foreign Counterintelligence
FOSO	Field Operation Support Officer
MCWFO	Marine Corps West Field Office
NCIS	Naval Criminal Investigative Service
NCISRA	Naval Criminal Investigative Service Resident Agency
NIS	Naval Investigative Service
NISO	Naval Investigative Service Office
NISRA	Naval Investigative Service Resident Agency
NISRO	Naval Investigative Service Regional Office
NISRU	Naval Investigative Service Resident Unit
ONI	Office of Naval Intelligence
OSI	US Air Force Office of Special Investigations
PSI	Personal Security Investigation. Same as BI.
RDO	Regional Director for Operations
RRA	Representative Resident Agent
SA	Supervising Agent or Special Agent
SAC	Special Agent in Charge
SARDO	Special Assistant to RDO
SDFO	San Diego Field Office
SRA	Senior Resident Agent
SWFO	Southwest Field Office

24
Contributors

Bud Aldridge, Pete Anderson, Brandon Armstrong, Mike Barrett, Tom Boley, Mike Bourke, Tom Brannon, Joe Brant, Chuck Briant, Ron Bright, Larry Butler, Dick Childs, Tom Clark, Wayne Clookie, John Davies, Nina Drammissi, Bill Eade, Kevin Edge, Larry Ferrell, Dan Foley, Earl Fowler, Vince Giaime, Steve Gutshall, Kathy Hampton, Bob Helbock, Bill Herzig, Ted Hicks, John Hopeck, Al Hughes, Ron Janson, Ed Jex, Michael B. Jones, Steve Kahl, Ray Larabee, Al Larson, Ron Larson, Henry Lingen, Al Marretta, Jack Marine, John Marquete, Grant McIntosh, Brian McKee, Vic McPherson, Cheryl Mencel, Ted Miller, Roy Mosteller, Kelly Murphy, Jerry Nance, Joe Naylor, Bill Nugent, Ken Oglesbee, John Olson, Bob Panico, Toni Perrin, George Reis, Harry Reeves, Earl Richey, Pete Riley, Harry Rogers, Lou Sanchez, Jewell Seawood, Dan Simas, Cliff Simmen, Bruce Smart, Art Spafford, Harry Stovall, Doug Stuart, Dick Sullivan, Doug Tomaso, Wendell Taguchi, Dennis Usrey, John Wagner, Richard Warmack, Chuck Warmuth

Underlined names are believed to be NIS Plank Owners

25
About the Author

Allan Sipe was raised in the Los Angeles suburb of Monrovia. He went to schools through High School there before going to California State Polytechnic College (Cal Poly) and graduating with a BS in Technical Journalism in 1964.

Allan then entered the US Navy Officer Candidate School and received his commission as an Ensign in the US Navy Reserve in 1965. Following his matriculation from the Defense Intelligence Academy, he was assigned to the Naval Investigative Service (NIS) in Vietnam where he served from 1971 to 1972 as a Lieutenant NIS Representative in Danang, Advisor to the Vietnamese Navy Security Bloc (Vietnam counterpart of NIS), and as a Counterintelligence Officer at the NISO in Saigon.

Following a two year assignment on the staff of Commander Naval Forces Europe, Allan separated from the US Navy after nearly ten years of service.

He accepted employment as a Special Agent with the Naval Investigative Service in July 1974. His first assignment was to the NIS Resident Agency (NISRA) North Island in San Diego. During the next two and a half years, Allan worked a variety of criminal investigations and served six months as Agent Afloat onboard USS Constellation (CV-64).

After two years with NIS in Okinawa, Japan, Allan returned to San Diego in 1979 with an assignment to NISRA Point Loma. During the next three years, Allan was detailed to a subordinate office at Ballast Point Submarine Base and also as a dedicated fraud agent at the Naval Supply Center San Diego. In 1983, NIS Headquarters was provided funding in order to commence a dedicated program in Foreign Counterintelligence (FCI). Allan was selected to be the first FCI Squad Supervisor in San Diego in charge of a four-person group.

In summer 1984, Allan was transferred to NIS Headquarters, Suitland, Maryland and assignment to the Counterintelligence Investigations Division. The highlight of the next two years was Allan's duty as Headquarters Case Agent for the John Walker espionage investigation in which he was the sole NIS agent involved in the debriefs of John Walker.

After selection for promotion to GS-13 in 1986, Allan was assigned as ASAC for FCI at NISRA Naval Station San Diego where he supervised the activities of six Special Agents and one Secretary. During this tour, the US Marine Corps Sgt Lonetree investigation prompted formation of the Bobsled Task Force in Washington DC to investigate numerous Marine Corps members suspected of security violations. Allan was selected for this assignment which turned into a four month detail. In 1989, Allan transferred to NISO San Diego to become the Assistant Regional Director for FCI.

In 1992, Allan was ordered to assignment as a staff officer with NIS Area Command Pacific Office in Hawaii. This office was responsible for liaison with the Commanders of US Forces Pacific and US Naval Forces Pacific. When this NIS Office was disestablished, Allan reported to NISRA Pearl Harbor as ASAC for FCI.

Allan returned to San Diego once again in 1994, this time as a member of the FCI team until his retirement from NCIS in December 1995.

CPSIA information can be obtained
at www.ICGtesting.com
Printed in the USA
FSOW04n1001290717
37005FS